"*The Bear Is My Father* is good medicine. Ultim[...] deceased man; Bear Heart is here—a living ancestor who resides in the hearts of those he touched. These pages retain the essence of his teachings, much like a drop of water taken from the ocean is still part of the ocean. This is a superb companion to the original *The Wind Is My Mother*, and I recommend they be read together for maximum impact."

— Glenn Aparicio Parry

 Author of *Original Thinking: A ReVisioning of Time, Humanity, and Nature* and *Original Politics: Making America Sacred Again*

"What a heart-felt, uplifting, inspirational book! Much more than a memoir, Bear Heart's own amazing story is amplified by memories and testimonials from his Medicine Helper and wife, Reginah WaterSpirit, and other friends and colleagues. Sprinkled with humility and humor, *The Bear is My Father* offers profound insights for best living, and remarkable examples of the intersection of science and the world of spirit."

— Anne Hillerman

 New York Times best-selling author of the Leaphorn-Chee-Manuelito series

"Bear Heart and Reginah gift us with a glimpse of the nature of the Indigenous Spirit of healing, well-being and loving-kindness in their story of a life well lived, and becoming a complete man—an authentic Indigenous Elder!"

— Gregory Cajete

 Professor of Native American Studies and Language Literacy Sociocultural Studies at the University of New Mexico

"*The Bear Is My Father* is replete with humor, wisdom, inspiration, and most of all, celebration of life and love. Reading this masterfully architectured book, you will know Bear, you will know your own heart, and you will know a man about whom not enough can possibly be written—Bear Heart, Keeper of the Sacred Wisdom of the Muscogee Creek Nation, healer, and storyteller who lives on not only in the Forest of Spirit but with us here in the Land of Seeking."

— Rabbi Gershon Winkler

 Author of *Magic of the Ordinary: Recovering the Shamanic in Judaism*

"In *The Bear Is My Father*, Bear Heart has given us a path into the spiritual wisdom inherent in the Indigenous experience, by illuminating the deep Native American traditional perspective that everything is connected and related, and all is divine vibration."

— Basil Braveheart
   Lakota Elder and author of *The Spiritual Journey of a Brave Heart*

"This very important book on Bear Heart's life and wisdom helped me get to know and see the many seeds of healing sprouted from this Native elder. Filled with many personal stories and teachings from Bear Heart, Reginah, and many others who were touched by his life, this book is a much-needed medicine to help us find our way in our world today."

— HeatherAsh Amara
   Author of *Warrior Goddess Training* and *Warrior Goddess Wisdom*

"This is a book that subtly transforms its readers. Read it and let it teach you. This is a different way of learning. Learn from this book gently and effortlessly. You may not even know what has happened but it has—trust it!"

— Sidra Levi Stone, PhD
   Author and the co-creator of Voice Dialogue

"Even if you never had the privilege of meeting Bear Heart or hearing him speak, you will feel his warm presence when reading these stories and get a feel for the depth of the man. The pearls of wisdom found in these pages can be spiritual guideposts for a good and fruitful life. I urge you to take a few steps down the path of this book and discover how much we all have in common."

— Doug Alderson
   Author of *Seminole Freedom* and *The Vision Keepers: Walking For Native Americans and the Earth*

"Bear Heart's wisdom is profound and lasting, but more so is his love that lifts and inspires you on your own journey to learn your own ways. Bear Heart sought to help others find strength through their struggles and purpose in their lives. How lucky we are to have his words to guide us, needed now more than ever."

— Laura Baker
   Author of *Stargazer* and *Legend*

THE BEAR
IS MY FATHER

THE BEAR IS MY FATHER

Wisdom of a Muscogee Creek
Caretaker of Sacred Ways

— Marcellus Bear Heart Williams —
& Reginah WaterSpirit

Edited by Tim Amsden

SYNERGETIC
PRESS

Synergetic Press | 1 Bluebird Court, Santa Fe, NM 87508
& 24 Old Gloucester St. London, WC1N 3AL England

Library of Congress Cataloging-in-Publication Data is available.

ISBN 9780907791898 (hardcover)
ISBN 9780907791904 (ebook)

Book design: Brad Greene
Title page art: Bev Doolittle
Cover photography: Kyle Malone, Kinfolk Branding
Interior fan photograph: Gene Sovo/Sia Collection
Managing Editor: Amanda Müller
Project Editor: Sage Wylder
Printed in the USA

TABLE OF CONTENTS

*Among my people, we carve the bones of animals
in such a way that they speak to us, and we speak
to them. I sing to the bear, and he guides me.
Can we not make room for the bear to roam free,
at least in some part of where we live?
Is he not our grandfather?*

— Bear Heart

Marcellus Williams and Bev Doolittle, 1992.

FOREWORD

— Bev Doolittle —

I first met Marcellus Bear Heart Williams at a Sacred Circle Ceremony in Yellowstone National Park about a year and a half after the great Yellowstone fires in 1990. I had created a painting for release as a limited-edition print called *The Sacred Circle*. My art publisher, the Greenwich Workshop, had arranged for this special gathering to be filmed as a short documentary to be released with the print.

My painting consisted of nine panels that fit together like a grid. Each panel represented a different environment in North America, from the smallest creature (a frog) to a large grizzly bear snatching salmon from a river. All the white elements from each panel are connected into a circle around the center panel depicting a Native American astride a horse, who represents "man" and his ability to change the balance of our ecosystems. We must learn from nature; Mother Earth is our teacher.

The purpose of the Sacred Circle Ceremony was "to call on the hearts of people to rekindle a true appreciation of all life forms." Bear Heart, who conducted the ceremony, explained: "We set up the circle and allow people to come in and share our appreciation, to ask the Great Spirit to bless what we are trying to do, not only for ourselves today but for those that follow after us, for those not even born yet."

Bear Heart's words deeply resonated with me. I felt privileged and thankful that he would become a significant part of our project, and I came away from that day knowing I would not be the star of this film. I'm happy to communicate through my art, but Bear Heart became the voice of that production, his words linking each segment into one beautiful whole.

I've been an artist all my life. Communicating visually takes a lot of practice. Watching people and observing nature is a learning process, but that's only half of it. Those interactions and relationships provide a depth of understanding that allows the artist to communicate to others honestly and with compassion. I've been lucky that the things I love—the things in this world that inspire me to paint—are loved by so many others. That connection is invaluable, but the main driving force behind my artwork is a primal urge to make an image that's meaningful and true.

This is also the way of Bear Heart's artistry. When I met Marcellus for the first time in Yellowstone, I was immediately enthralled by his special art form; the way he communicated verbally with such ease, sincerity, knowledge, and purpose. The poetry of his words and his message were uniquely his. His influence will always be with me, as it will be for so many others.

In Yellowstone, I was busy absorbing the visual of us just being there, sitting around the campfire at the end of the day, when with a sweeping hand gesture Bear Heart said to me, "In what you are doing, you are keeping all this alive. You may think your canvas is inanimate, but what you put into it speaks for itself. It cries out, 'Look at me, look at me! See how I am full of life, in harmony with the landscape! When you paint a grizzly, you're sustaining the life of my father and of my father's relatives because I am of the Bear Clan. My father was of the Bear Clan. I regard all bears as my father." Now every time I view *The Sacred Circle* painting, I remember Bear Heart, that special day, and how much I needed to hear his words.

By nature, I am shy and introverted. On the other hand, when it comes to duty, I am like a bulldog. Creating a painting takes time, thought, and years of skill-building. Often it took weeks or months to complete one of my paintings.

While I was in the creative process, I was in my comfort zone, but after I had completed a painting, it was part of the marketing process for me to travel around the country and make appearances at galleries, give speeches, and interact with customers. One-on-one was doable but speaking before an auditorium full of people—yikes! Grading myself after an event was a little game I played, which was not a negative exercise at all. I enjoy challenges, and I'm always open to self-improvement. Sometimes my son and husband played along too, and I valued their input.

One day, just before giving a presentation to an audience full of customers in Carmel, California, I thought about the ease with which Bear Heart spoke. He was just himself, every word coming from the heart. I realized I needed to take a page from his book. I was standing in the dark with a mic, giving a slideshow about myself and my own art. Really, how hard could it be? If I put my foot in my mouth, so what? The bulldog in me rose up, and I delivered. I spoke for an hour, and I got an "A."

I feel blessed to have made friends with Bear Heart and his wife and medicine helper, Reginah WaterSpirit. Our paths have crossed many times over the years. One time they came to stay with us in Joshua Tree, California, and on another occasion, my sister-in-law, Teresa, and I drove out to Albuquerque to visit them for a few days. We were invited to an all-night Native American Church ceremony on a friend's property just outside of Albuquerque. The exacting rituals, the tipi, the singing, the drums, the peyote, and even the rising sun in the morning all contributed to an unforgettable experience. I didn't have to understand all the words of their prayers, but I certainly felt them.

Another time, we were all invited to a Greenwich workshop publisher's seminar to be held in downtown Vancouver, where Bear Heart would be the keynote speaker. While we were there, I asked him if he would pose for me for a painting I was working on, called *Prayer for the Wild Things.* All he needed was a blanket, his eagle feather headdress, and a length of tubing to give him something to hold up above his head as if it were a ceremonial pipe. I brought my camera, and my husband found an empty conference room where we did our photo shoot.

Bear Heart's keynote speech, as expected, was a major hit, and he was asked to reappear the next day. The event went perfectly, and all was well. I learned later from my publisher that Bear Heart had lost his wallet while on his way to the airport for his departing flight. He got back home to Albuquerque, and I do wonder how he pulled it off. In today's world, he'd still be in Canada!

When I read Marcellus Bear Heart Williams's book, *The Bear Is My Father*, I am again in Bear Heart's presence, touched by his wonderful, insightful life lessons. The fun, pathos, his own considerable frankness, and the stories of Reginah WaterSpirit are endearing. It's also a joy to see him through the stories of others whose lives he graced.

Being with Bear Heart is as close as I can imagine to being touched by a spirit. I think of him often and treasure those first days when I met him in Yellowstone when we marveled at how the wilderness can renew itself and how well nature's creatures can adapt. His rich, deep voice resonates from these pages with passion and purpose, as it did when I was with him. He was a scholar of the soul and a speaker for the heart. *The Bear Is My Father* is a beautiful book that speaks volumes.

— Tim Amsden —

Bear Heart was a man of contrasts. Although he was not physically large, his presence and sonorous voice filled the room. He was highly educated, but his words—like the fundamental truths they carry— are clear and simple. He was a Native American who grew up in a world where he and his ancestors were subject to persecution and prejudice, but he never projected anger or resentment, only forgiveness, and peace. As they said about Will Rogers, he loved people; he never met a man (or woman) he didn't like.

Today, we need his counsel. There has never been a time when the spiritual principles of Indigenous people are as essential for the world, for living in harmony with each other and the living earth. Fortunately, we have the spirit and words of Marcellus Bear Heart Williams, among those of other Native people, to help point the way.

Bear Heart's broad education and participation in the wider world of cultures and ideas makes him unique among Indigenous medicine people. He studied for 14 years under two medicine men of his tribe, had an undergraduate degree, a divinity degree with a major in Biblical Greek, and an honorary PhD in Humanities. He was a World War II veteran and served for seven years on the advisory board for the Institute of Public Health at Johns Hopkins, where he represented Native American people.

He prayed with President Truman, spoke at the opening of the Smithsonian Native American Museum, and gave spiritual counsel to firemen and their families after the Oklahoma City tragedy in 1995. He served on President Bush's Faith-Based Initiative Panel for the US Department of Health's "When Terror Strikes" conference in

New York and put down prayers with police and firemen at Ground Zero in New York City.

Bear Heart gave the keynote speech at the World Shamanism Conference in Garnish, Germany, in 2000. He traveled extensively throughout the US and internationally, lecturing, healing, teaching, learning, and sharing his gifts. He was a roadman in the Native American Church, an American Baptist Minister, and a multi-tribal spiritual leader. He spoke in 14 languages, 13 of them Native. His first book, *The Wind Is My Mother*, was translated into 14 languages.

This book was first written before Bear Heart passed and shelved. Then after his death, it was re-edited and expanded. It is a three-dimensional portrait of Bear Heart, through the eyes of Reginah Water-Spirit, his co-author, wife, and medicine helper, and others whose lives he enriched. It is also the story of a beautiful and unlikely relationship between one of the last traditionally trained Native American medicine men and a Jewish woman who was born in New York City and created garment-related businesses in Southern California.

The lives of my wife, Lucia, and I were deeply enriched by the many years we have known Bear Heart and Reginah. Years ago, they honored me by asking that I edit this book in its original form, which I eagerly did, and I agreed again when Reginah asked me to edit it in its current iteration. With great help from Lucia and Reginah, it has been re-organized and expanded with the inclusion of much more material, so it can better serve as an expression of the legacy of this extraordinary and unique human being.

In my own writing, I have occasionally felt as if the spirit of someone else were there with me, guiding my thoughts and my words, but never as consistently as with this work. I could almost continuously sense Bear Heart pushing me along, saying "yes" to this and "no" to that, and hear his warm chuckle. Hopefully, you will feel him too.

Editor's Note: This book is written by Bear Heart and Reginah Water-Spirit, with stories from various contributors included within many of the chapters. Both Reginah and contributor's names are listed prior to their entries. All other writing is authored by Bear Heart. As you read through this collection, you will begin to noticeably differentiate between each writer's unique voice and the lessons they have to share.

SECTION I

BECOMING
BEAR HEART

Marcellus Williams at four years old.

CHAPTER I

GROWING UP CREEK

I was born on April 13, 1918, in Okemah, Oklahoma. I am a full-blooded Indian from the Creek Tribe, Muscogee Nation. I am 87 years old, and I'm still here for a reason, but I don't know what it is. There must be something more that I am here to do.

My father was traditional, and my mother was a devout Christian and leader in the Baptist Church, so I grew up learning both Christianity and the traditional ways of my people. I also learned Creek medicine ways from two teachers who chose me when I was 18 years old. Their names were Daniel Beaver and Dave Lewis, and they came from two different clan lineages. I studied with them while attending the all-Indian Bacone College in Muscogee, Oklahoma, and I continued to study with them for many, many years.

The story of my people is that a very long time ago, a heavy fog rolled in and surrounded everybody and everything. People gathered together in groups, in different places in the fog. The animals and birds were scattered among them. One day a wind came from the east and blew the fog away. One group was near a field where they had been planting potatoes, so they became known as the Potato Clan. Others were named after animals that were among them when the fog lifted: Bear, Bird, Deer, and so on. The group that was in the east had no animals or birds, so they became known as the Wind Clan because the wind that blew the fog away had come from that direction. That's how clans came into being in our Tribe.

To be a member of a clan is to have particular responsibilities— for the self, for the clan, for the society as a whole. The Bird Clan must respect the air. The Wolf Clan must respect the property of others, of what we call the two-leggeds, or people. The Bear Clan is a protector of not only their own family but others as well. Bears are known to walk around a camp to see if there's anything harmful.

There are many, many ways in which clan members fulfill their responsibilities. The common responsibility the clans share is respect. So, the first thing for you to know about me is that my mother is of the Wind Clan, and my father is of the Bear Clan. That tells you something right there.

My great-grandmother, Yebie, died on the forced relocation called the Trail of Tears when she and others were made to march from the southeastern part of the United States to Indian Territory, which is now the state of Oklahoma. Our people were forced by our own government to leave Alabama and Georgia and walk all the way from there to Fort Gibson in Indian Territory. Soldiers on horseback herded them, kept them moving. They left their farms (our people were agriculturists), their homes, their crops in the fields—everything. When people died along the way, no time was allowed for decent burials. They dropped the bodies into ravines and put rocks or sticks over them and went on.

My great-grandmother died because her feet had frozen. She had been forced to walk in the snow with no shoes. This is not somebody else; this is my own flesh and blood. I could have lived all my life with animosity in my heart against the government that forced our people to do that, but my Christian mother taught me at an early age that forgiveness is best. Even though what they did wasn't right, we must learn to love. We may not forget, but we won't let it stand in our way of having a good relationship with all people.

After we settled into Indian Territory, a great leader of my Tribe was a man called Chitto Harjo. His name means "Crazy Snake," and he fought against our land being divided into private pieces. He knew that breaking up the land meant it would be sold bit by bit to people outside the Tribe and become lost to us. He hid out in the hills near what is now Eufaula, Oklahoma.

One of the things that we don't talk about is the Little People, the imps who live among us. They can make you get lost, even in your backyard. That's what they did with the soldiers who were looking for Chitto Harjo. They made those soldiers go around and around and around. When the soldiers finally found the entrance to the big cave where Chitto Harjo was hiding, they were met by big snakes. They could never get in, so Chitto Harjo was never found, never captured. If he had been, he would have been forced to sign a document or make a statement that would have had bad effects on the government and the lands of our Tribe. He didn't want that, so he stayed hidden. He was never found.

My brothers and sisters were much older than me, so I had to learn how to get into mischief by myself. I grew up on a farm and learned about farming things—plowing, building little levies across the land, picking cotton and ears of corn. I remember at night filling my tub, taking a bath, getting into my nightclothes, and going to bed. When you get through working on the farm in the evening, my, what a peaceful rest you have! You don't lie there tossing and turning. You know everything that's going to happen will come in its own time, so you don't lie there worrying about it.

Early in the morning, I'd go out and get a fresh bucket of water, light the fire in the cookstove for my mother and get the eggs. Then I'd go back, milk the cows, and feed them with the hogs and horses. Then I'd wash up and eat breakfast and walk almost two miles to the country school. I've never regretted all that. Spring came, and you could wear tennis shoes or go barefoot. I did both.

In those days, most boys learned how to be hunters. We had to develop patience and our sense of observation. We noticed what time of the day particular animals came to drink. Did they come alone, or were they in pairs? Did some watch for danger while others were drinking? When they left, did they take the same route they used to come, or did they take another route? If a flock of birds rose suddenly, did something scare it? Was it a man or some other kind of predator?

In order to hunt, you don't just go somewhere and start looking. You find a good place and stand very still and slowly move your eyes, watching the periphery of your vision. You don't make any sudden moves. When you are walking around while hunting at night, you have to learn to do it as quietly as possible. In places where there is no grass, but there are lots of dried twigs, you put the ball of your foot down first and then lower the rest of your foot carefully, so you won't crack anything and make noise. If there are tall weeds instead of twigs, you put your heel down first.

Sometimes a particular day would be set aside to go hunting. There was a man who was in charge of the hunt, and he would meet the hunters at a certain spot and send one group east, one south, one west, and one north. The man in charge of the hunt was called Master of Breath because he was sending the people out so that game could be killed—deer, squirrel, rabbit. Master of Breath is also our word for the Christian God. He gives breath, which is life, and he can take it away.

Some of us also learned about being a warrior. A good warrior just takes essentials with him. He doesn't strap a computer on his back and carry batteries in both hands—he takes his weapon and goes forward.

He never fights in anger because if he does, he's lost the battle. He respects the person he's fighting. He relies upon all the bits of knowledge that were given to him and learns how to put them together to focus on the immediate challenge. In many cases, he relies on the subconscious without even realizing he is doing so. He knows that his subconscious is the storehouse of all his experiences and that it holds the knowledge he needs to solve his problems. He relies upon that, and it comes through. He allows his subconscious to work with his conscious mind. That's how many problems are solved.

Even in Christian churches in our Tribe, we carried on our traditional ways. Men sit on one side, and women sit on the other side, as we did in the dance area. The Native preachers were not seminary trained, but they could really quote the scriptures and preach in our own language. Boy, some were really good preachers! I guess in many non-Indian churches, seminary training is a prerequisite. In ours, all you have to know is your belief in God, accept His Son as the Messiah, and never run down anyone whether they are Methodist, Presbyterian, or anything else. We used to have a lot of Methodist preachers who came to preach in our churches. My home church was the Greenleaf Baptist Church; I grew up there. My mother was a strong backbone of that church.

One time when a man was preaching, instead of saying, "The devil," he said, "The one that wears the red coat. Be careful. He can lie. He can trick you. He wants to steal your soul. So be careful of the one in the red coat." Just then, a Methodist preacher came in late through the back door. He came in wearing a red blazer!

In our church, after the sermon, they put chairs in front for people who wanted to accept Christ or to sit in if they have felt like they had sinned and wanted to ask for forgiveness. Many of our pastors, not being trained, asked a lot of personal questions about the situation of the sinners seeking forgiveness. On one occasion, a man came up, and the preacher asked, "Why did you come?" The man said, "I have sinned." The preacher asked, "In what way?" and the man said, "I guess you could call it adultery." The preacher asked, "Was the other person a Christian also?" and the man answered, "Yes, I think so." The preacher asked, "Is that other person in this room?" and the man replied, "Yes, I think so." The preacher said, "Point out this person," and the man did. It was the preacher's wife! The preacher just looked at him, yelled, "Damn you!" and jumped on the man. The deacons had to come and pull them apart. The preacher was going to fight him. So, I guess there are some disadvantages to not being trained.

We had what we called the stick ball game. There was a pole with a board on top shaped like a fish and a little ball made of deerskin. The men had ball sticks that were forked at the end, with a rawhide net in between. The women could use their hands to catch and throw the ball. When someone hit the board, it was one point. There were score sticks for both sides, and when one side scored, the scorekeeper would take away a stick from the other side. When one side was out of sticks, the other side won. I guess our stick ball game was the forerunner of lacrosse.

There were people, kind of like referees, who admonished the players during the game. If you had the ball and someone tried to knock it away from you by sliding their stick down and hitting your hand, they would be admonished. If something like that happened and you fought back, it would mean you're not worthy of being called a man, and you would be admonished. What you should do if you are hurt is give a war-whoop and turn around four times, and then continue to play. That's what a man does.

The ballplayers would be painted in three colors: yellow, red, and black. You got painted with yellow, so if you got hit with a stick, it wouldn't keep you from playing. The color absorbed the pain, and you went right on. The red paint was so that if your skin was cut and you were bleeding, you could keep on playing. And if you got a broken bone or something else serious, the black would absorb it and make sure that you got safely out of the game. The colors weren't put on just to be painting; each color had its meaning.

The night before the game, the women of one team would gather with the women of the other team. They'd each bring something to bet that their team would win, and they would tie together whatever they were betting with a long string. Then they would sing all night long.

We had big tournaments where the two teams who had won the most games would play each other. At one of the tournaments, one man was hit above the eyes, and it tore the skin in a long line, and the skin flapped over his eyes. There were spectators from all over, and some were government officials that stopped the game. Later on, they prohibited that kind of tournament because they were so rough. We still play the stickball game after our all-night ceremonies, but it's a friendly game.

Because of my mother's Baptist religion, she didn't let me play, but I watched a lot of games. I had a cousin named Major Dixico. He had an Indian name, but Major was his English name. He was a great ballplayer; nobody could stop him. Sometimes there would be two people hanging onto him, trying to get the ball away from him, and he'd still score.

CHAPTER 2

PROTECTING HIS HEART

My father's final illness and his death came from pernicious anemia. Because it happened in the hot summertime, I built a brush arbor outside the house and put his bed there.

I would sit up all night under the arbor with my father. The lantern would be going, and I rubbed his back with a certain medicine and read the Bible and prayed. He had renewed his Christian faith, and sometimes I'd sing some songs to him from our own hymnal. The 40th chapter in Psalms talks about people who don't come to see you anymore. You feel alone and abandoned, yet God is still with you and knows who is faithful. That was his favorite verse. I would read it over and over.

I had to remain alert because when someone is about to go across, there are witches who want to come around and steal the heart. They are kind of like vampires—they use hearts to extend their power. My elders used to say that when they visited someone who was suspected of being one of those witches, they would look for a tiny iron pot. That's what they cooked the heart in. Anyway, in order to protect a loved one who's about to go across, you must stay alert all night, and that can be difficult because we have a way known as long-distance hypnosis, where a person can put an entire houschold to sleep.

Long-distance hypnosis was given to us before we ever came to Oklahoma when we were back in Georgia and Alabama. It was used for hunting when there was very little game. Our hunters would put the animals they were hunting in a trance-like state so they could get what game they needed. They never took more than they needed, and they always gave an offering for the life they took. Later the gift was misused to put people to sleep to rob them or take advantage of them in other ways.

Before someone who had hypnotized people left the house, they scratched the sleeping people with a thorn, just a little bit. When they got a certain distance away, they hollered, and the sleeping people stirred in their beds. That way, the spell was broken, and the people in the house would wake up naturally when morning came.

There were several ways you could have your house doctored to protect it from long-distance hypnosis. One was to take a particular kind of feather and put it over the doorway. If someone tried to send hypnosis to the house, the feather fluttered, and the sound woke the people up.

Some witches could shoot a foreign object into a person's body, where it would fester and cause pain. Even if we had x-rays in those days, they could not have seen it because it would move around in the body.

When I sat up all night looking after my father, I kept his loaded 45 pistol with me all the time. One of my mother's relatives, who was a medicine man, came by and said, "I hear that you've been sitting up at night, taking care of your dad. I'll fix some medicine for you to use to stay awake. Nobody will be able to put you to sleep. Also, I'm going to fix your bullets. If a witch comes, their eyes glow kind of like fire. When you shoot at them, you don't have to aim. The bullet is fixed, so it'll be guided to that person."

I put the bullet in the pistol and was sitting there one night when I saw a light going this way and that in our graveyard, not too far away. I knew it was a witch watching me, wanting to get my father's heart. I got up and walked toward the light, pointed the pistol, and pulled the trigger. The gun clicked, and I pulled the trigger again. It clicked, and I pulled the trigger a third time, and again it just clicked. While this was happening, I could hear the witch laughing at me, "Heh, heh, heh." The fourth time I pulled the trigger, and the gun fired, bang! I heard "Oooh!" and I went back to my dad. He didn't say anything. He knew what I was doing.

In the morning, some of my lady cousins came over to help my mother clean the house. We were the only Indians in the area that had a telephone, and we were on a party line. Our ring was two long and two short: "bzzz, bzzz, bz, bz." The phone rang for us, and my mother answered. The person calling was an Indian woman that was using the phone at a neighboring man's house. She said, "My mother fell off the wagon and hurt herself. I need some kind of medication and thought maybe you might have some over there." They knew that we went to town often and kept a lot of things on hand. My cousins said, "Tell her we'll go and bring them some things that might help."

When my cousins came back, I overheard them talking to my mother. "She didn't fall from a wagon," they said. "She was shot." She later died, and that left me wondering, did I kill her? And then my cousin, who was one of the deacons of our church, came over and said, "You can protect your loved one. That's all you knew to do, and you were doing that. You didn't go out to hurt her. You were defending your father when she came to you. So don't think there is any guilt on your part."

We are given many gifts, and we can use or misuse them. The gifts themselves are not what matters; it is how they are used. We make a choice to use this or that gift and decide whether or not to use it in a negative way. In our Tribe, we had many medicine women and men who practiced dark things. It seems like every Indigenous tribe knew about some forms of witchcraft and how to protect and cleanse themselves from them.

All of these are choices we make. The Creator allows us to make our choices. We are going to answer to Him for everything we've done on the last day. He will say to us, "I allowed you to have certain gifts. Tell me how you used them." That's my teaching on that.

When my father's time was near, my mother said, "You'd better go and tell your aunt." She lived several miles away in another county. She was older than my father, and she was blind. I drove to her house that night and told her, and her daughter and her husband, who lived with my aunt. They said, "We'll have our prayer here tonight, and we'll come first thing tomorrow."

As I passed a bridge west of our house on my drive back, the dome light in the car came on. I knew it wasn't an accident; the switch was way up beside the light in that car. Then the light went out by itself, and that's when I knew that my dad was gone. We had a boy staying with us, helping me to do things around the house. When I drove up to the house, he came out and said, "You just lost your father." But I knew already. I knew my father was gone.

Some of our relatives had come over that evening after I left. I later learned that they were all sitting around praying when at the very last moment, my father lifted his hand and pointed. With a great smile on his face, he said, "Jesus, Thy will be done."

I was 12 years old when my father died. He was put into the ground, and before the dirt was shoveled in, we each threw on a clod of dirt. Then people took shovels and helped fill the grave and handed them along to other people to let them help as well.

After he was gone, I felt a great sense of emptiness. I would cry myself to sleep on top of his grave, and some people that came and stayed with us for several days would take me back into bed. A medicine man on my mother's side came and doctored me, and I finally got all right.

Later on, a friend of the family came and built a small shelter over the grave. We do that to all our graves. I was surprised when I took a trip to Europe and went through a museum which contained Viking ships and other things from their culture. There was a little building that looked like our grave houses, and I asked if that's what they used to put over their graves. The answer was yes, and I was also told that, like us, the Vikings would prepare a dish that a dead person liked and put it at the gravesite. There's a story about a white man who saw an Indian doing that and said, "Hey, when is that dead person going to come and eat that food?" The Indian looked at him and answered, "The same time that your dead come up to smell the flowers that you put on your graves!" As I said, my father had renewed his Christian faith, and once, before he was bedfast for good, we went to church. When we came back, he said to my mother and me:

"I closed my eyes during one of those songs when everyone was singing. When I opened them, all I saw were flowers everywhere. I closed my eyes again, and when I opened them, there were the people singing. It came to me that none of them had more than an eighth-grade education, but it didn't matter. When you know God and have him in your heart, that's what really matters. Those people had their faith and their song."

My father said that in our language, which is very expressive. When we try to say the same thing in English, it just doesn't come out the same. I received many of my teachings from my father, traditional ways as well as general things to live by. Many of my father's teachings still come back to me, here and there.

World Fancy Dance Champion
21-year-old Marcellus Williams.

CHAPTER 3

DANCING SACRED AND COMPETITION

Long ago, my people were looking for Tookebudche, and they found a tall, ordinary-looking man. They asked him who he was, and he said he was Tookebudche. They told him, "We heard you are very powerful. Show us your power." He said, "All right, but I have to holler four times."

On his first holler, the grass began shaking. When he hollered a second time, the leaves on the trees began shaking. On his third holler, the trees began shaking. On the fourth one, even the ground itself was shaking, and he said, "This power comes from on high." And so today, our people have the Stomp Dance to honor Tookebudche. It's called the Stomp Dance because during the dance, you stomp—you hit the ground with your feet.

The Stomp Dance is danced by many tribes, and it is hundreds of years old. The place where the dance is performed is called the stomp ground, and it's a somewhat sacred spot. Of the 44 original Muscogee stomp grounds, I'd guess there are about 12 that are still in use. Most went out of existence as many of my people have become Christians and given up the old ways.

The town with the stomp ground that my father belonged to was a long way from us, and the one that was close to us was my mother's stomp ground. Membership in a stomp ground is from the mother's clan, so I was a member of my mother's stomp ground. If you marry a woman from another stomp ground, you are allowed to participate in her stomp ground as an in-law.

When you are first initiated into a stomp ground membership, you are scratched by a medicine man four times with a thorn, maybe on the calf of your leg or on your arm muscle area. The four scratches (which never become infected) indicate the four hills of your life. The first hill is growing up from being a child. The second is when you get married. At the third hill, you have children of your own, and the fourth is when your children have their own children, your grandchildren.

At each stomp ground, there are four dances a year. The first is when the earth puts on its green grass and new leaves; that's our New Year, so the first dance is to give thanks for another year. The ashes of the fire from the last year's dance are scattered over the stomp ground before the first dance.

The second dance is for people who have been in war and come back. They have been in places where blood has been shed: World War I, World War II, and Vietnam. The blood that was spilled has a tendency to bother their dreams and health. They take medicine that's been fixed for them, which enables them to endure and survive in a good way. An elder tells them, "You didn't die because you have something to do for the people to help them in some way. There was a reason behind the fact that you weren't killed. You were meant to live for a certain purpose."

The third dance is for the renewal of the arbors on the dance ground. There are four arbors made of willow branches, one facing east, one facing west, one facing south, and one facing north.

Our greatest dance is the fourth one when we fast for the corn. We're not allowed to eat corn until we've fasted for it, taken medicine for it.

Before the fourth dance, the men take an emetic medicine and fast, to clean themselves out. The emetic is made from a red root called "The Fire," and it's known as the king of emetics. We take it because we are going to perform before the Great One. The emetic medicine is also sprinkled all the way around the edge of the stomp ground, and the women cannot cross the line where the medicine was placed. The women come up to the line and are given the same emetic medicine. They fill their buckets and take them back to their own camps and clean themselves out as well.

Next, the men have a sweat in a sweat lodge built near a stream. After the sweat, the men jump into the stream and submerge four times, cleaning themselves outside as well as inside. If a man gets weak, it might be because he's been close to a woman in her period. He has to go back into the sweat lodge four more times, then dip in the water four times again.

People come from many different places, some from areas that have their own stomp grounds. Most bring their own groceries, but whoever comes will be given food and a place to camp.

In the afternoon before the ceremony begins, the medicine man goes out on the north side, and a spokesman tells all the visiting campers, "We have now come to the quiet time. Please control your children. No loud laughing or talking. Now is a very special time to allow communication with the Great Creator." Everybody keeps quiet as the medicine man spends a long, long time standing out there, communicating with the Creator. When it's over, the spokesman tells everyone, "Now you can talk and let your children play."

When the ceremony and dancing are ready to begin, the women have a place of their own to sit, separate from the men. All the arbors are filled with people from the area, and visitors sit in the spaces between. The chief of the town sits in the middle of the dance area, beneath a shade structure made of poles with willow branches on top. Sitting on his left-hand side is his spokesman, who is called Heneha, and right behind them sits the medicine man of the town.

Whatever the chief wants the public to hear, Heneha will tell them. As an example, Heneha might say for the chief:

"I have sat here many times with other elders. We used to visit, dance together, take medicine together, but one by one, they have all gone. Now I sit here, cloaked in a robe of loneliness. But by you coming here, as I hear the children laughing and playing, you have lifted up my heart. I greet each one of you. Thank you for coming. When the ceremony starts, I want you all to take part. Let us come together as one people and celebrate what has been left in our hands to carry on. I want you and your whole family to enjoy yourselves. Let us enjoy ourselves together throughout this night."

It's a speech unlike any other. The spokesman doesn't have to think about it at all; it just comes, and he says it in a singsong kind of style. Two men control the dance. One of them selects the first stomp dance leader, and the dancing starts. During the dance, the two men go around, kind of like deacons of a church, and see that no unnecessary talking happens during the dance. What they are doing is honoring the dance and the dancers. After the first dance is over, one of the two men appoints the leader of the next dance. He announces, "I have chosen the leader. When he comes down, we want all of you to join in and help him."

The dance songs are antiphonal. The leader sings, the group answers, back and forth, "Yo, Yo," then the answer, "Hey!" When you get through, you holler at least four times because, in the beginning, Tookebudche had hollered four times.

The women have terrapin shells with holes and little tiny rocks inside. They tie them above their ankles and move their feet to keep time. My sister still has a set of those turtle shells, even though she never danced with them. That's how the ceremony goes on all night. We also had other kinds of dances. In the Duck Dance, couples, men and women, hold hands. Three couples in front raise their arms in arches, and those behind them kind of wobble like ducks as they go through. When they get through, they arch their hands and form their own arches, and others go through them. It's a fun sort of dance.

We would sometimes dance about things we didn't like, such as too much alcohol. In the Drunk Dance, people danced like they were drunk and couldn't stand up straight. The Drunk Dance song says, "People are going to say he's drunk again." By honoring the power of drink, you are better able to keep it from capturing you in addiction. It helps you be strong enough to push it out of your system and your mind.

The Stomp Dance and these other dances are all just for members of the tribe. Some are sacred, and they are performed for our own culture and purpose. Other dances, like those at Pow Wows or for shows, are done for competition and entertainment.

Fancy Dancing began when William F. Cody, known as Buffalo Bill, started his Wild West Show around the end of the nineteenth century. They called him Buffalo Bill because he killed 100 buffalos in one day. They never did tell us what happened to the meat or the hides.

Cody invited Ponca, Pawnee, and Otoe Indians to dance as part of the show. Indians don't perform their ceremonial dances for entertainment, so they created Fancy Dancing. Gus McDonald, a Ponca, was one of the greatest Fancy Dancers—he led the others in the show they put together for Buffalo Bill.

In 1938, at the Indian Exposition in Anadarko, Oklahoma, I entered the Fancy Dancing World Championship Contest. My name was not Bear Heart then. In those days, I traveled with boys from Otoe, Pawnee, and Ponca. They used to call me Buckskin.

Fancy Dancing takes a lot of stamina—you have your full costume on, and they judge you on your body movements, your head, how smoothly you turn around, back and forth. You had to end your dance on the very last beat of the drum with both feet on the ground. I used to end by doing the splits.

They had all kinds of things there: the pipe dance, the chicken fluttering dance, and the feather-picking contest. They'd dig a hole and put a feather in it, with just a little end sticking out. While you were dancing, without skipping a beat, you'd try to pick it up with your mouth. You couldn't use your hands.

That was in Osage County. The Osage had a lot of money then because they pooled all their resources together, and the head of each family was given a check every month. One man got my attention and said, "Come here." He had dug a hole, and instead of a feather, he had stuck in a twenty-dollar bill. "Pick it up, and it's yours," he said. Boy, I was going to pick up that twenty-dollar bill if I had to use my hands, but I did it right and picked it up with my mouth.

Anyway, they took the best fancy dancers from a lot of different Pow Wows. I was one of the five finalists, and we danced over and over again. I won the World Fancy Dancing Championship, and they gave me five hundred dollars and a trip to Madison Square Garden, where I performed as the featured specialty—the Native American Indian dancer from Oklahoma.

During my performance, there was a Russian ballerina in the audience named Lisa Parnola. She had never seen American Indian fancy dancing before and was very impressed with what she saw. Lisa and I talked afterward, and I showed her some of my steps. She tried to get me to go back to Russia with her.

I told her I couldn't because I was still in school, and I had to get my education. She said, "Any subject you want, we have people who can help you get your degree." I told her I had other things to do and to get a degree like that would be too easy. I wanted to earn my education. Also, Russia was still under the communists at that time, and they might have forced me to be a spy for them. I'm glad I never did go down that road.

She invited me to her ballet performance and gave me a ticket. At the end, during her encore, she performed some of my steps. I was real proud about that.

Bear at Inipi site. Illustration by Bear Hear

CHAPTER 4
MY NAME

My name, Bear Heart, Nokus Feke Ematha Tustanakee, came to me when I was in my mid-20s, during my fourth vision quest outside of Bear Butte, South Dakota. During that vision quest, I was visited by a bear—not a vision of a bear but the real thing. The bear came over to me and stood up on his hind legs, which they do when preparing to attack. I stood up and faced him, and he knocked me down, gently for a bear, and I got up. He knocked me down again, and again I rose and faced him. I talked to him in Creek. I told him that my father was of the Bear Clan and that I wasn't going to fight him, but I wasn't going to run. He listened, turned around, and walked away.

My teacher, a Cheyenne elder, told me, "You have the heart of a bear that respects strength, and you are not afraid to stand up to

him." The experience was so powerful that he gave me the name Bear Heart, and I took it openly as my own. It's natural for members of the Bear Clan to have names related to the bear. There are names like Bear Paw and Bear Foot, but as far as I know, I'm the only one in my Tribe that has the name Bear Heart.

If you are named after a bird or animal, it's good to know something about your namesake. The bear is very psychic. He knows and distinguishes various things in the forest. He has poor eyesight, but he has insight that can see deep into things. The bear is big, strong, and heavy, but he can run through the woods and never break a twig. He is as gentle as he is strong.

When a bear goes into the water and then comes out and shakes, all the individual sparkles of water reflect the sunlight. When he shakes his head, the bear is sharing his powerful mental processes with all living things.

The bear teaches us about taking care of ourselves before we get sick. Every winter, the bear goes into his den and hibernates. That's the healing period that allows him to function better when he comes out of hibernation. He shows us that there is time for everyone to rest and not overdo it. Most of us don't follow that wisdom.

The bear is very protective. He moves in and out, through the mind, body, and soul, to see that everything is on the up-and-up. His presence can be reassuring and fill us with confidence that we're on the right track. That's my feeling concerning the bear.

MEDICINE HELPER

Reginah WaterSpirit and Bear Heart, 1994.

CHAPTER 5

BECOMING WATERSPIRIT

— Reginah WaterSpirit —

I was born into a Jewish family in the Bronx, a borough of New York City. According to the Gregorian calendar, my Earth birthdate is August 23, 1942, which by the Jewish calendar is 10 Elul 5702, Yom Rishon, a Sunday. The Mayan calendar has me fixed at yet another date. At this writing, my age is 77, but American Indians and some other cultures would say I am older because they count the gestation period.

The path of my life has woven through the creation of several unique businesses in the garment district of Los Angeles, education in consciousness studies, and immersion in Indigenous spiritual beliefs and ceremonies. All along the way, I have been centered in art; I see my world through the lens of a philosophical artist, searching for meaning and beauty. Sometimes I am unable to communicate my experiences in words, especially those that are "other worldly," so I paint them. I once found myself inside a scene I had painted 15 years before, which surprised even me.

In 1979, I boarded Queen Elizabeth II in New York harbor to cross the Atlantic Ocean bound for Europe. After traveling from the Netherlands to the Greek Islands, I settled down for almost two years in Italy, where I painted in a 14th-century structure supposedly inhabited by Machiavelli as he wrote *The Prince*.

When I was 42 years old, I began a quite different life with Marcellus Bear Heart Williams. We traveled in the United States, Europe, Mexico, and Canada for 23 years. At first, I served as his medicine helper then became his wife. Bear Heart greatly expanded my awareness of Indigenous spirituality, which enhanced my teaching of psycho-spiritual disciplines. During that time, I also reconnected with my Judaic faith, which was really always there.

I first got to know Bear Heart through a friend in Los Angeles who was an assistant psychology professor at UCLA. He was a Frenchman who had taken Bear Heart as his adopted dad. He would come to my condominium overlooking the Pacific Ocean in Santa Monica and say, "Reginah, you're depressed. You need a sweat lodge with Bear Heart. You need a vision quest." I would usually respond, "I'm not doing anything with you or your friends. You're all into some crazy stuff."

At the time, I was studying Voice Dialogue, a discipline that former Jungian analyst Dr. Hal Stone and psychologist Dr. Sidra Stone had co-founded. Because this method helps people get to know themselves in unique and profound ways, it helped me to stretch into "unchartered waters."

My French friend was aware that I was studying Voice Dialogue, part of which is based on the ways of Carl Jung. One day he said, "You know, the Jungians are coming from Europe to study alternative healing methods with Bear Heart, and they're going to be in Santa Fe this weekend." I said, "Oh, the Jungians are coming?" and he knew he had me. I went out and bought an airplane ticket. We flew to Albuquerque and drove up to Bishops Lodge in Santa Fe.

After we arrived, we began preparing for the events that would come, including helping to build a sweat lodge. I tried to be very respectful as they cut willows for the sweat lodge and put tobacco down. I stood there holding willows while they said, "The willow is giving its life for a bigger purpose," but I was thinking, "Okay already, let's get to the Jungians." The Jungians finally arrived, and of course, they didn't want to hear all the details of what I was learning. They were there to be with an old Indian medicine man.

When Bear Heart arrived, he walked directly over to me, pointed to the sweat lodge, and said, "You're coming in, aren't you?" The word "yes" flew out of my mouth before I could think to catch it. We went in and sat in a circle with me close to the exit flap and Bear Heart across from me. A man with a pitchfork brought in hot lava rocks and placed them in a pit in the center. Someone closed the flap, and it became totally black. As the heat increased, I felt engulfed in a wave of fear.

Bear Heart began to sing in an Indian language. I had been holding my breath, but as he sang, I relaxed and began to breathe deeply. He was giving some kind of instruction, but I was not paying attention. I kept hoping I was going to be able to handle the heat and wondering what exactly was expected of me. Soon the person on my right touched my shoulder and said, "It's your turn." Without much thought, I said, "I hope I make it through the first round." That was my first prayer in an Indian way. It wasn't profound, but it was very honest, and I did make it through the entire lodge.

After the lodge, we all had dinner at the home of Bear Heart's relative. When the meal was over, I went into the den and was falling asleep when Bear Heart came and sat down close to me. He told me that my prayer was one of the sincerest he had heard in a long time, and he appreciated it very much. I didn't know what to say or think. He was very respectful, but it occurred to me that he was either a very kind man or flattering me for some reason. It took me years to see that maybe both were true.

Later that evening, Bear Heart asked me to come to Albuquerque and help him with his work. He was 67 years old, and I was 42 years old. I was thinking, "What kind of work does he do?" I couldn't imagine that the things he did at the gathering were his work because it didn't look like work according to my background in the garment industry. I was unaware that in addition to being a traditionally trained medicine person, he was an ordained American Baptist minister. I didn't know what he was asking of me, but at that point, I was sort of retired. I had sold my businesses in Los Angeles, had an income, and was secretly daydreaming about moving away from California. Within three months of his invitation, I left the West Coast and moved to New Mexico. I believe my experiences with Voice Dialogue opened me to accepting that turning point with Bear Heart.

When I arrived in New Mexico, he invited me to his home. It was almost Thanksgiving, so I offered to prepare dinner for him and his family. On Thanksgiving morning, I drove to the address Bear Heart had given me, a simple four-bedroom house on a double lot in a semi-rural part of Albuquerque. I had all the fixings to make a special traditional Thanksgiving meal. My mother always had a magnificent Thanksgiving dinner, so I was planning a seven-course feast.

Bear Heart's family helped me bring the supplies into the house, but Bear Heart himself seemed to be out of town, which was a bit shocking to me. I got to work roasting the turkey and making the other dishes and tried not to look disappointed.

After several hours and well past the time to serve dinner, I began to wonder if I should continue to wait for Bear Heart. It was four o'clock, and I had told him we'd be ready to eat at two. The family didn't have any knowledge of his whereabouts, or if he planned to be home at all, so I finally announced that it was time to eat. Some six adults, three young grandchildren, and a few other relatives and friends came to the table. As they were getting ready to offer a prayer,

Bear Heart came rushing into the house, walked directly to the head of the table, and took off his cowboy hat. He offered a prayer but never expressed an apology or explanation for his tardiness. His behavior left a lasting impression on me; in my world, people who are late apologize.

I expected people to sit down and begin to eat, talk, and visit. Instead, each person filled their plate to the brim and walked away from the table to watch TV in another room. There were TVs in most of the rooms, and they were all showing football games. Bear Heart motioned to me to follow him down a narrow hallway to his office, where we began eating our Thanksgiving dinner with pleasant conversation, but then things rapidly changed.

Bear Heart's nine-year-old grandson, Bobby, came to the office door and said, "Grandpa, men are here to see you." Bear Heart left the office without a word, and I sat there with my plate on my lap. When he came back, about a dozen men were following him, and they all lined up in the narrow hall. I thought I should leave, but Bear Heart motioned for me to stay put. There wasn't really room for me to get by the new visitors anyway.

A Native man had apparently been incarcerated for possibly killing a law enforcement agent, and these men were there to pray for him. Bear Heart led them in a prayer that he told me later was called a flesh offering. He handed each man a pipe, and while they prayed, some in a low voice and some silently, he took a tiny piece of skin from their upper arm with a sewing needle. He wrapped each piece individually in red cloth and handed it back, with instructions to bury it near their houses. Then the men ate what was left on the table, shook everyone's hand, and left. I had never seen or imagined such a way of offering a prayer.

It was a very strange holiday for me. I was unaware of how very different the ways of traditional Native families were from my own.

I learned that in Bear Heart's culture, every day was a sacred day for which to be thankful. Over the years, Bear Heart joked that Native Americans were invited to the first Thanksgiving dinner at Plymouth Rock but, for some reason, were never invited back!

Over time, as more grandchildren arrived in Bear Heart's family and marriages and relationships became more culturally mixed, his family and friends observed mainstream American holidays more. But most of them also kept their tradition that every day is a new and sacred day. I shifted in that direction. I began to give less credence to being grateful on just one day a year and took on the practice of noticing the blessings each day brings. Bear Heart (who liked to play with words) would say, "It's a good day to live." instead of the war cry, "It's a good day to die."

I had been in New Mexico a short while, Bear Heart was traveling, and I was setting up my new place to live. I decided to visit an adopted daughter of his in Santa Fe, and while sitting in her living room listening to her CDs, I came across a very catchy tune. The artist was Jimmy Pepper, a musician and singer with a unique style of contemporary Native music. As I was singing along with him, Bear Heart's daughter corrected me, "You've got that wrong," she said. "You're saying 'woe is me,' but the words in the song are 'water spirits.'" I checked, and she was right. The lyrics were: "water spirits swimming round my head, makes me feel glad that I'm not dead." After some discussion, we called to see if Bear Heart could shed some light on the words.

He did and told us that those lyrics were alluding to the medicinal plant, peyote, used in the Native American Church all-night ceremonies. I knew Bear Heart was a Roadman in the Native American Church, which is what the leader of their ceremonies is called, but I was not familiar with the use of the term "water spirits" to refer to peyote. I told him I didn't know peyote could make a person grateful to be alive or, as the song put it, "glad I'm not dead." Then he turned to me, smiled, and asked, "Well, what would you like to be called, 'Woe Is Me' or 'WaterSpirit'?" I said, "I may be a little down, but I'm not stupid. I think I'll go with WaterSpirit."

That's when I first got my Indian name. I also call it a nature name to remind myself of my connection to all living things, especially those that flow like water. I didn't use the name for a long time because I hadn't really earned it in a traditional way, but years later, I met an Indigenous woman who helped empower other women on their path in life. She worked a lot with water, using it as medicine, and during my time with her, I spent many hours standing in the cold flow of the Chama River near Ojo Caliente Resort in northern New Mexico. I was praying to be able to express myself in meaningful ways when I saw little beings dancing on the water. I looked closely and saw that they were made of tiny waves at the river's edge. After sharing this "vision" with Bear Heart, he said, "You have now earned your name, 'WaterSpirit.'"

Some years later, Bear Heart and I were in Oceanside, California, in a second-grade classroom as guest speakers. Hanging from the top of the whiteboard was a sheet of brown wrapping paper with questions for Grandfather Bear Heart and me. Included was a question I often get, "How did you get your name?" and as usual, I didn't give them the whole story, just a short, simple answer, "Water in a river just keeps flowing on. I always try to keep flowing forward, no matter what happens. So, my name is WaterSpirit."

After many years with Bear Heart, I began to pay more attention to the little things happening around me. For instance, sometimes, he would wake me with his singing in the middle of the night, often with the song, "Ol' Man River." After I had heard it several times, I wondered if it contained a message for me, especially the words, "Ol' man river, that old man river, he just keeps rolling along." Then

I thought about what I had told those second graders. Maybe I did tell them an important part of what the name means for me. Keep going no matter what, don't let obstacles stop you. It's a thought that has helped sustain me during some hard times.

CHAPTER 6

HELPING HIS MEDICINE

— Reginah WaterSpirit —

Bear Heart began introducing me as his "medicine helper," which made me a bit embarrassed. I thought, "What exactly is his medicine?" I knew nothing about the herbs he was using or the techniques he employed. I watched him make medicine by blowing air into water through a drilled eagle leg bone, and it seemed like a trick. I had no idea how deep, complex, and ancient his traditional medicine was or how hard he worked to keep all his chants, songs, and procedures fresh in his memory.

When Bear Heart was asked how he made his medicine, he always answered, "I don't make the medicine. It was here before me. I've been entrusted to be a caretaker of certain sacred ways." He said he didn't decide to become a medicine man; Bear Heart was chosen by his elders when he was a young man. He couldn't just quit doing what he did because of the vows he had taken.

A medicine helper is very different. We could get out of the job if we wanted. I wasn't chosen, I was invited, but others might have been invited who could have done a better job. There are many medicine helpers around Bear Heart and other elders, and they often have specialties. Some medicine helpers are good at ceremony and learning the songs. They help with prayers and teaching the rituals that support well-being and spiritual growth. Even though they may not claim the title, many people are medicine helpers because, although they work at a regular job and have a family to care for, they always show up to help build a sweat lodge, buy food, and do whatever else they can to provide support.

My friend, Theresa Maudie, once asked Bear Heart to do something for her and her family, and afterward, she handed him a donation and said, "Your prayers are priceless, but I want to help with the cause." To me, that is helping with the medicine. Sun Bear, Bear Heart's younger brother and medicine chief of the Bear Tribe Medicine Society, always said "good medicine" when he saw something positive, such as seeing me helping Bear Heart. It always made me feel acknowledged.

It takes a willingness to listen carefully to be the kind of medicine helper I was because you are not always given specific instructions. I learned to be silent and listen with my ears and my heart to what was needed. Sometimes it was just for me to get out of the way, or sometimes it involved learning a lesson that I didn't know I needed.

Early in my medicine helper training, Bear Heart took me to visit a lady suffering from Bell's Palsy. The entire right side of her face was distorted. Bear Heart, who never told me beforehand what I'd be asked to do, instructed me to get a washcloth. After he spoke to the lady about never going out for a walk in the wind because things travel around that cause us harm, he prayed aloud and sang a chant. He then blew bubbles in water with the eagle bone, gently used the water to wash the lady's face with the cloth, and repeated the process three more times. The last three times, he asked me to wash her face. I found myself being very careful, very gentle as if I were washing the face of a baby. I was very surprised at how good it felt to be helping another person in this mysterious way, both empowered and humbled. We returned three more times to see that lady, and she got much better, almost well.

I related this experience to my mom, and she told my aunt, who also suffered from Bell's Palsy. My mom and my aunt bought Bear Heart and my airplane tickets, and we were off to Palm Desert, California, to make medicine for my aunt. We stayed long enough to do the four sessions, and she got even better results than the first lady. My family began calling me the Indian's medicine helper, but I knew I still had very much to learn.

One of the important things I had to do was learn more about myself and look at the parts of me that I would rather not admit exist. At one point, I almost quit the job because I realized that I didn't like most of the people who came to Bear Heart for help. I was frustrated and sad because I didn't know how to turn my negative feelings around, and I confided my concerns to a very close adopted daughter of Bear Heart, Shelley Dominguez. It seems obvious now, but as I complained to her about those people who kept coming to Bear Heart to fix their lives, she said something I can't believe I didn't understand. "Reginah," she said, "Why do you think they come to Bear Heart?"

I was judging those people as arrogant, needy, and having no self-respect, rather than seeing that they needed someone who had enough patience to continue loving them until they were able to connect with a loving Creator. Then another light bulb went off in my head—I realized that I was one of them! Even though I was helping and doing whatever I could to be of service, I needed to carry the same uncritical accepting love. Oy Vey!

I began to look at myself and other people in a different light. I thought about something I had learned from my beloved teachers of Voice Dialogue, Drs. Hal and Sidra Stone: understanding and learning about yourself is a process, not an event. Honoring the values and beliefs of our own numerous personalities gives us a chance to be more accepting of others. We all deserve the medicine and care for our spirits that we need. People from all kinds of situations came to Bear Heart for help. I had to stay open-hearted to deal with each one and have patience and love for them, as well as for myself. Humor especially helps. I noticed one day that the initials for the name I had before I became Reginah WaterSpirit, Regina Newell, are "RN." That is sort of funny.

Humor was also an important part of Bear Heart's medicine. Most people don't realize that he had an excellent eye prosthesis in place of his left eye. He lost his left eye in an accident at the age of 14, when he was trying to fix his mother's iron bed frame with a hammer, and a piece of iron flew into his eye. His missing eye was the basis for a couple of experiences we had together when I was driving (I did a lot of driving) that helped me understand myself better and shift my attitude.

At one point, I was very annoyed with Bear Heart because he kept making me go out of the way to avoid making left-hand turns where there were no signal lights. I kept telling him that I didn't have a problem making left turns, but he wanted me to work it out so that unless I was at a stoplight, I rarely turned left.

One day I decided to close my left eye, so I could experience what the world looked like to someone with only one eye. There was little depth perception, and when I drove, I had to turn my neck constantly, so I felt very vulnerable. It was very hard to think of going through life that way. I decided that if it was more comfortable for Bear Heart, I'd do it his way.

Bear Heart read a book a day when we were home, but my eyes got tired after a chapter or two. When I complained about too much reading or that I couldn't find something, he would sometimes say that I had too many eyes.

Another time I was driving Bear Heart and his adopted Navajo brother, Denny Sandoval, to a Native American Church meeting in northwestern New Mexico. Denny Sandoval was blind but very perceptive and spiritual. He had been taught by Bear Heart about the difference between inner perception and blindness a long time ago, and that started him on a different path in life. So, because Bear Heart had only one eye, even though there were three of us in the car, there were only three good eyes, and I had two of them.

Well, I guess Denny could tell how proud I was, driving those two spiritual leaders up to the meeting, so he paid me a compliment about my service that made my head swell up even more about what a great thing I was doing. As I drove, flush with feeling very "in charge," storm clouds began to form, then lightning and rain began—lots of it. We often joked about the many orange barrels used to designate construction zones on the highways here in New Mexico, sometimes saying they are the official state flower. Those barrels started showing up everywhere, the road narrowed to one lane, and the storm intensified.

Visibility was pretty much zero, but Bear Heart, in his mid-70s at the time, took the wheel. Almost immediately, the sun came out, the orange barrels disappeared, and the road widened. I thought, "Good, I'll drive now." As soon as I took the wheel, the pouring rain returned, the road narrowed, and lightning almost hit the car. After a while, we switched again, but the storm and bad road conditions again disappeared. Bear Heart, of course, said it was just another situation where I had too many eyes. I thought that maybe it happened because I was feeling too self-important, believing the weather beings would only cooperate with us if I was driving.

In those days, I tended to be very self-critical, which I covered up by acting like a know-it-all. Accepting criticism, even when it contained valuable lessons, was always hard because I felt so criticized from within. Bear Heart would say that "Some people know so much that they don't have any room to learn anything." That's how I was with criticism. I was so self-critical that I didn't have room to learn.

But sometimes, it's easier to learn from the elements than from people, and that was true for me that day when I learned something about humility from the weather. I didn't feel as criticized as I would have if the lesson came from a person. During my years with Bear Heart, I began to accept my own value as a human being, which allowed me to be more appreciative of my self-worth and place in the scheme of life.

After I had known Bear Heart and his family for a few months, I had to return to central California to see my family, and I spent three days with my brother, Warren, in his home in Reedley, California. Before I left New Mexico, Bear Heart gave me a blessing for safe travel and for things to be good for my family. As he was giving the blessing with his eagle feather, he said, "I'll send a dove to communicate long-distance with you." I guess he knew I needed that continuity of communication with him, and he was doing everything he could to keep the lines open. I just nodded, thinking, "A dove?" and mumbled, "Yeah, sure."

As I was walking around my brother's neighborhood, I came across my brother's neighbor as he watered his lawn (who had lived there a long time) and I noticed the cooing of a mourning dove. I said to him, "Oh, you must have a lot of doves here." He said, "No, we don't get any doves in these parts," so I asked him to listen carefully. When he heard the dove, he ran into the house and brought his wife outside and told her to listen. They were both surprised to hear a dove cooing. After I arrived back in New Mexico, my mom called to say that I had a message from the neighbors. They said to tell me that since the day I left, they hadn't heard another dove.

That incident, like the storm during my drive with Danny and Bear Heart, was another interaction with nature that helped me suspend my disbelief and open myself to healings for which I longed. A real feeling of connectedness with all living things had never before been present in my life, but I now know that birds are part of who we are. Bear Heart is related to the Bird Clan through his mother's clan, the Wind Clan, and I am related to the Bird Clan through one of my vision quests. I have several Indian nature names, one of which is "Adopted by the Bird Clan."

Another wonderful bird experience involved an egret. In August 1990, my beloved mom, Ruth, was preparing to cross over. She was in Eisenhower Hospital in Palm Springs, California, and I slept in the room with her a few nights before she made the crossing. I had already learned from Bear Heart that the egret comes to carry the soul into the next world. I had been praying that things would be gentle for my mom and that she wouldn't be in pain.

Although there is a huge lake and bird refuge in the area, it is many miles southeast of the hospital. I had lived on and off around there for 20 years, and I had never seen an egret in the vicinity of Palm Springs. Very early one morning, I woke up next to my mom and looked out the window at the first crack of light, where a large white egret was patiently sitting on the railing of the hospital room's balcony. My breath stopped, and I heard an inner voice that said, "It's time." My mom crossed over very soon after the egret arrived.

I guess you could say it was a coincidence, but out of all the balconies at Eisenhower, this egret landed at my mom's window. My mind is so strongly based on "reason" that even today, I have a part of me that says, "You were dreaming." or "It's not significant." My reality, however, is that the large bird was there for a reason, and I am grateful for the love and support of a beneficent Creator.

My mom had a very loving relationship with Bear Heart. He was in New Mexico when she crossed over, and when she died, he called to let us know that mom had come to him. The nurse told me that Bear Heart's call for me came in at the same time my mom passed on. If we are open, we learn that these kinds of things are normal and show how our appeals for loved ones to the Creator can be heard. Bear Heart would say, "People look for the spectacular, and they miss the point."

Two months after 9/11, Bear Heart served on a faith-based initiatives panel for a big conference for all the human services departments in the country. There were hundreds of people there: social workers, psychologists, spiritual leaders from different belief systems, and first responders. The conference was called "When Terror Strikes" and focused on the problems of coordination among agencies and others involved in responding to terrorist attacks.

We were flown to New York and put up in the Downtown Hilton. Tommy Thompson, Secretary of Health and Human Services at the time, gave a talk, then the meeting moved into discussions of how we could respond in better and more coordinated ways. They focused on such basic things as putting responders together. They could talk and get to know each other so that when a disaster happens, strangers aren't dealing with strangers.

While we were there, an adopted relative of Bear Heart came over and offered to take a small group of us down to Ground Zero. We agreed, but when we got to the area, there was a big crowd waiting to ride little golf carts down into Ground Zero itself. The New York police and firefighters immediately noticed Bear Heart because they didn't usually see Native Americans in their 80s wearing cowboy hats walking around in Manhattan—although I guess they were used to seeing everything else.

They evidently recognized that something significant was happening. They brought us up to the front of the line and got into a little tussle about who was going to take Bear Heart down into Ground Zero and how they were going to get our whole group into those little golf carts that only seat four people. They talked about it for a few minutes and then brought over a long cart that seated eight to ten. After they decided who was going to drive it (it was a policeman), we got in, and they took us down to the platform they had built to view the site. My first impression was surprise that the rubble smelled like it was still smoldering.

Earlier, on the way to Ground Zero, Bear Heart had asked me to pick up several white roses from among the great number that had been laid around the area. When we got to the platform, he asked me to take the petals off the roses and start handing them out to our little group. I started pulling off the petals, but when I lifted my head to look at our little group, it had become a huge circle of people, including policemen and firemen, who were all standing quietly. Almost everybody had stopped what they were doing and joined the circle in dead silence.

Bear Heart said to me, "Now, pass the petals out." I passed them all the way around, surprised that I had exactly enough. Then Bear Heart offered a prayer and sang a song in Otoe, his own language. The song was a going-on song addressed to those who had died there, with words that meant, "Go on, go on, don't look back, someday all of us will follow, and we will be together forever, not just for a short time." Then he instructed everybody to drop their petals. We all followed Bear Heart's instructions and just let those petals float down. It was a very powerful moment.

As I said, I am of Jewish heritage. I've been to Germany and seen signs to Auschwitz and other concentration camps, and they gave me a very eerie feeling. That's how Ground Zero felt. I had watched weeks of extensive television coverage, but I hadn't noticed that the buildings had been draped in enormous sheets of black cloth. Although they were 40 or 50 stories tall, buildings all around the area had been draped along their entire sides because they had lost their windows. The eeriness of those black cloths, combined with the cold and damp, made it seem like we were on another planet. Everything was dark and black. When I think back about that day, I see Bear Heart bringing in our small group, gathering everybody else up, tying us all together, and helping us shine a beacon of light into that terrible darkness.

Bear Heart had an adopted daughter, Della Warrior, who was President of the Institute of American Indian Arts (IAIA) in Santa Fe, New Mexico. Della would occasionally call me up saying, "Reginah, do you think my dad could do this or do that?" and I always tried to arrange things, sometimes at the last minute. She was always very grateful, and they had a really beautiful relationship.

One day she called me about the 40th anniversary of the IAIA. Bear Heart and his adopted brother, Raymond Butler, had prayed and put down Indian tobacco years and years ago for the IAIA to have its own buildings—they used to be located in the barracks of the College of Santa Fe. Today, of course, they have a magnificent campus, so she really wanted Bear Heart to be the grandfather in the 40th-anniversary parade in Santa Fe.

It wasn't possible, though, because he had to be in California during that time to sponsor a Native American Church meeting. The meeting had been arranged a year in advance, and there was just no way he could not go. I was beside myself because I thought I'd have to tell her I couldn't help, but fortunately, all of a sudden, the idea sparked in my head that perhaps Bear Heart could be represented by his older sister, Lucy Gibson, who would be in New Mexico during that time. I called Della back and said, "I can't deliver Bear Heart, but I can deliver his 90-year-old sister and three of Bear Heart's granddaughters." So, on the day of the parade, I drove Lucy and three of Bear Heart's youngest granddaughters up to Santa Fe.

I had the girls bring their shawls and some nice Indian clothes, and when we arrived, we saw a long line of brand-new Sebring Chrysler convertibles along the side of the square. The parade organizers asked me if I would be the driver of the car that would carry Lucy and the girls, and I said, "Sure." He pointed out our car, which had a big sign on it the school had made that read, "Descendants of the Trail of Tears. We are still here."

I placed Lucy in the front seat beside me and the kids sitting up on the back, where they looked sweet and beautiful. We got in line and started driving around the square, and people were lined up along the side of the road. I saw them looking at the sign and then at Lucy and the kids and then looking back at the sign again. I realized something very powerful was happening.

The people were surprised because they knew that the Trail of Tears folks had been pretty much wiped out. So many died on the Trail(s) of Tears—and I talk about the trails in the plural form because there wasn't just one. Many American Indian groups were forcibly marched from their homelands, and many died.

All of a sudden, the people watching the parade realized that they were seeing an elder woman and her grandchildren, who had family on that terrible trail. They started clapping, just a few at first, then slowly faces lit up throughout the whole crowd, and everyone began to clap.

Lucy was deeply touched, but the kids didn't know exactly what was happening. So, I gave them a history lesson on the way home. Now, if you ask those girls, "Who was your ancestor who died on the Trail of Tears, they say "Yebie." They know her name, and they know she is their third great-grandmother.

One day, years later, Lucy's son, Jack, was in the hospital in Albuquerque. Jack was near passing over, and I was at a loss as to what to do for Lucy, so I took her across the street to the 66 Diner for lunch. When the aroma of the food hit my nose, I absent-mindedly said, "I'm starving." Lucy got very quiet, and when we sat down, she simply said, "I don't think so." Her people knew what it meant to be starving. Her great-grandmother died on the Trail of Tears. I try now to never use that phrase, no matter how hungry I am. I guess the history lesson I gave to the girls about their ancestor who died on the Trail of Tears came back home to me.

Bear Heart's eagle walking stick. Photograph by Kyle Malone.

MEDICINE WAYS

CHAPTER 7

OUR STORIES
WEAVE TOGETHER

— Nina Brown —

When everyone should've been in bed at three o'clock in the morning, I rode on the shuttle to the Albuquerque Airport. As most of the other passengers slept, the man seated next to me and I began a conversation. His name was Nick, and we chatted about this and that. He told me he had just attended a medical conference and how deeply impressed he had been by one of the speakers, a Native American Shaman.

As he talked, my mind wandered back to a book I had read, *The Scalpel and The Silver Bear,* by Lori Arviso Alvord, MD, the first member of the Navajo Nation to become a surgeon. Dr. Alvord wrote about nurses and doctors being in spiritual harmony with their patients in the operating room and how much more successful the outcome was when all participants in the room were at peace on the spiritual and physical level. Thoughts rushed into my head about how wonderful it might be to have a speaker present insights like those of the Navajo surgeon to the medical staff at Los Alamos Medical Center where I worked so that our doctors might reach beyond their medical school training, adding to their expertise and caregiving in other ways. I asked Nick if he could somehow find that special speaker so that my vision might become a reality. That's how it began for me—the miracle of Bear Heart.

Several months later, on December 11, 2002, Bear Heart was seated at the front of the room in the United Church in Los Alamos, New Mexico, cloaked in his ceremonial dress, totally appropriate for the occasion of addressing the scientific and lay community of Los Alamos. Cameras were focused, the audience was eager, and all had been prepared for his words to be spoken. Then, when the moment was perfect, the leader of the second-largest business in the city stepped forward. As the host and CEO of the Los Alamos Medical Center, he stretched out his hands which contained tobacco and a gift, to honor Bear Heart. He held out his hands four times in the Native American tradition and then made his presentation to his esteemed guest. Quiet settled in as Bear Heart began speaking and found his pace. The audience, entranced, made not a sound. Bear Heart's words continued to flow and flow and flow. At the end, there were no questions, no applause, only quiet appreciation.

Bear Heart's talk was being filmed for a PBS documentary, and as the cameras and microphones captured the words and images of him, something else was also happening. In the audience sat a caregiver who oversaw all the inpatient services at the hospital. For her, the evening was eye-opening. For the first time, she saw in a different way. She later said she saw Bear Heart and the woman filming for PBS surrounded in a colorful aura; just these two were in her new focus.

At the end of the talk, with a tape of Bear Heart's "Medicine Songs of the Native American Peyote Lodge" playing, Bear Heart sat near the back of the room accompanying himself, chanting quietly as each person left, touched differently and uniquely, feeling and interpreting what they had experienced.

But Bear Heart had not completed his visit to the Medical Center. The next morning, he came to the hospital to meet with employees who had been unable to join him the night before. Each individual felt special when he greeted them and expressed great appreciation. The interchange of traditional and non-traditional was most apparent when Bear Heart asked for advice from one of the physicians at the hospital—a doctor who had listened to his wisdom the night before.

After the meeting, the entourage slowly moved through the corridors, into the elevator, and out onto the Medical/Surgical wing. Juanita was chosen to escort Bear Heart into each patient's room, asking permission first and then introducing the hospital's guest. Always with great respect, Bear Heart greeted each patient and family. With some patients, he chanted and prayed, quietly or aloud. With others, he had a conversation about healing and the needs of the body. The patient was always grateful, grateful for the love, and grateful for the concern.

When the visits were complete, Juanita suggested that Bear Heart might want to go to the Intensive Care Unit (ICU), where there was one more patient. This patient was in a coma and would not even know that he was present. "Yes." Bear Heart said, using just one word, as he often did. Bear Heart spent only minutes with this patient, not speaking except to acknowledge a family member who was close by the bed. His arms moved, and he was focused, and then he left. Goodbyes were said, and the hospital's special guest drove down the Hill to return to his home.

Several days later, while making his rounds throughout the departments and floors of the hospital, "Chief Greg," the CEO of Los Alamos Medical Center, met a family member of the ICU patient with whom Bear Heart had visited. The family member expressed her appreciation to the hospital for sharing with them a Native American healer who, in their opinion, had made a big difference in the life of her relative. The patient was no longer in the ICU. She had been moved to the Medical/Surgical wing very soon after Bear Heart's visit, and she was no longer in a coma.

One would think that the story of the visit of Bear Heart was complete at this point, but even to this moment in my life, the experience appears to be open-ended. The impact of that meeting with Nick in the shuttle to the Albuquerque airport continues. Reginah WaterSpirit and Bear Heart entertained me a few weeks after his visit to the hospital. I asked for advice at the end of my visit, for I wanted to bless the new home of my youngest son, Alex, who lives in Atlanta, and whose birthday I was also going to celebrate. Most of the answer was already known to me—that I was to use sage, an abalone shell, and a special feather. What was missing in my formula, which Bear Heart carefully pointed out to me, was to involve Spirit in the ceremony.

A few days later, my plane took off from the Albuquerque airport, taking me (I was somewhat nervous) to perform the blessing ceremony as my birthday gift to my son. I took a white feather from Honky, the albino peacock who lives in the tree above my 1940s adobe, along with a tightly tied bundle of sage and the abalone shell. This was to be a rare experience, sharing such intimacy with my son in this special way. But it appeared I was not alone. In the very large plane, which had many people on it, seated directly across the aisle from me, was a young man. The book he was reading at the time was on the floor, face-up. There was Bear Heart on the cover of his first book, *The Wind Is My Mother*. It was clear Bear Heart was coming with me.

On the night of Alex's 31st birthday, we stood together in the living room of his condominium as he unwrapped his gift. His permission was asked before we invited Spirit to join us in the special blessing of that most special space.

How does one understand something like this completely? Was Nick sitting next to me and Bear Heart introduced to me so that Joann could finally see her first aura or so that the ICU patient could come out of her coma? Was it so that my son, Alex, could live in a space filled with more love? I don't know, but what I do know is that listening to and believing in the voice inside of me as I headed down the highway was the beginning of a change in my life, and to some degree, the lives of others, and that Marcellus Bear Heart Williams was the reason for these and other changes.

CHAPTER 8

MY MEDICINE

For a long time, the medical profession attacked diseases as if they were at war, and they didn't consider the person that had the disease. They looked only at the disease because that was how they were trained. As modern medicine became more and more high-tech, many of the doctors became ultra-specialized. Their focus became even narrower, and the costs rose higher and higher. Without the doctors knowing it, people started turning away to other things that brought the same positive results at a lesser price. That's where alternative medicine and approaches came in.

Alternative medicine was seen at first as something bad by the medical profession, but as time passes, they are beginning to see that alternative ways really work. They are learning that many different things can help, and you must consider the person along with the disease. This is a big step toward understanding the kinds of treatment people need.

It used to be that when a man was in the hospital, the doctor just said to the nurse, "Do this. Give him a shot." The doctor didn't talk to the patient and tell him, "This is going to help you," to establish a positive response. The doctor was in power, and his only job was to treat the illness. If patients talked about how their illnesses were affecting their lives, the doctor didn't listen. But that is changing. Doctors are beginning to include the person, the way the person thinks and feels. Now they listen better to get a clearer picture of related things that go along with illnesses. They think more about how to treat the whole person and how to talk to the patient as a human being—not just as a machine that needs to be fixed.

Alternative medicines are becoming accepted. The medical profession is slowly discovering what many other people already know, like using homeopathy and essential oils to alleviate pain in some areas, such as the respiratory and nervous systems. We are also discovering that modern medicines often have serious side effects.

Doctors are becoming more aware of how important the mental and emotional parts are in illnesses—depression and irritation must be considered. But alternative medicine people still often know better how to handle the particular person and the best thing to prescribe. Medicine is more effective when it balances what's going on physically with what's going on in the mind and when different approaches to healing are included. There are many approaches to the practice of medicine today, and they all have something to offer.

Part of good treatment is considering what people have grown up with, their cultural background, and if they have folk medicine ways. Many people have a background in using plants for medicine. Some look upon these things as just folklore, and when the doctors hung out their shingles, they dropped everything they knew from their culture and said, "The doctor studied for this. He'll know best." But when things come up that the doctors don't understand, they don't have much to offer. It's easy to say, "You have a virus." but that doesn't explain anything; it just kind of lets things dangle along. When I come up against something for which I wasn't trained in my traditional ways, I remember that 80–90% of all illnesses come from the mind. What is required is to change the way a patient is thinking about their particular disease and inject positivity all the way through.

With research, many things can be improved, and we look forward to that, but it seems like the more we learn about one thing leads to another, and we have to address that in research as well. So, it goes on a never-ending process, looking for the magic bullet that will kill the disease. But there is almost never a simple answer. Good medicine is a combination of many things, taking the best of this and the best of that to alleviate particular situations. Diseases like Alzheimer's, Multiple Sclerosis, and problems with the spinal nervous system are challenges that take not just modern medicine but all the tools we have.

We have to consider not only the disease but how it affects the whole person. The curvature of the spine, for example, eventually affects other things, putting pressure on different parts of the body, such as the heart and the digestive system. We can't just consider one thing because the whole person is involved. We have to work on pain and the mind and consider the people around the patient, as well as try to correct what is physically wrong. We have to try to understand how it went wrong. These are the approaches that are needed today.

SEND THE AMBULANCE BACK

— Neal Rzepkowski —

Winddaughter held a gathering of the Bear Tribe almost every year, bringing teachers to help make it happen. On Saturday morning, during one of those events, around 10:30 am, Charles Lawrence and I were doing a workshop down by the water with a group of about 12 people. Bear Heart was conducting another teaching group, and Brant Secunda was teaching another.

While I was working with the group, someone asked for a doctor over the camp's loudspeaker system. I didn't hear it but saw someone running down to my group, saying that they were looking for Dr. Neal to come right away to the area in front of the cafeteria. By the time I got there, the nurse who came to the gatherings was there. An old man whom I had noticed earlier was lying on a bench unresponsive. Apparently, he had collapsed on the ground a short time before while he was talking to his daughter.

Initially, he wasn't breathing and had no blood pressure, but as I was getting ready to do CPR, he began to breathe. I asked for someone to call an ambulance. Within a minute or so of when I got there, Bear Heart and Brant arrived. Both had heard the call for a doctor, and both thought they were the type of doctor that was needed.

As I felt the pulse of the man, Bear Heart and Brant got ready to work. They looked at each other, and each started doctoring in his own way. Brant took his feather and worked on the man's solar plexus area and below, while Bear Heart worked toward the man's head.

As they were chanting and praying, I watched as Bear Heart cupped his hands together and pointed his fingers to the back of the man's head. This made a little "trough," with the hands pointing about four inches away from the area of the medulla oblongata. As Bear Heart prayed, he blew into his cupped hands. As I watched this, I saw three yellowish balls of light roll down the trough made by Bear Heart's hands and enter into the back of the man's head. Almost immediately, the man began to stir.

Shortly after, Bear Heart and Brant looked at each other and decided the doctoring was done. They quickly reassured us that all would be well and that the man would be fine. Neither stopped to make sure he had a pulse, nor did they speak to the man to see if he was okay. They simply stated he was now okay and then walked back to their workshops. They didn't hang around to see if there was anything else they could do or to take credit for what was done.

After less than a minute, the elderly man opened his eyes and asked why everyone was standing around him and staring as he lay on the bench. He sat up and said he felt perfectly fine. The nurse and I looked at each other, knowing that the only thing we could do was to make sure his pulse and blood pressure were okay, which they were. There was not much else we could do. The man's daughter was there and said her father was just as he had been half an hour before all of this happened.

In another six or seven minutes, the ambulance crew arrived, ready to take this man to the hospital for further evaluation. Now that they were there, looking at a perfectly conscious old man, we were in a dilemma about what to do. Western medical thinking would definitely recommend further evaluation in the emergency room. In fact, to send the ambulance away empty-handed required a release from legal liability if something did happen later. The daughter asked my advice.

What could I say? I risked malpractice if I advised against taking him to the ER. Yet, I believed with the same absolute faith of both Brant and Bear Heart that the man would be fine. I told the daughter that, as far as I could tell, her father appeared to be okay. I also told her about the lights I saw entering her father's head. She agreed with sending the ambulance away, and so we did! There were no further incidents at the gathering, and from what I have been told, the man continued to do just fine for at least many months afterward.

What we told the ambulance people must have seemed odd, but it was the truth. We had called them because the man had collapsed and was unconscious. While they were en route, two medicine men had "doctored" him, he regained consciousness, and he was fine. The medicine men said he was okay, and that was good enough for us. They were no longer needed to take this man to the ER. We signed the release of liability papers, and they were on their way.

❧ ❧ ❧

One of the first and greatest teachings stressed over and over again among my Tribe is the importance of respect. When treating a person for any kind of illness, whether it's mental, emotional, spiritual, or physical, we respect the person first as we try to determine the best treatment for whatever he is experiencing. We also respect the privilege of having been taught by an elder who passed his medicine ways on to us. We carry that respect every time we use their teachings.

Some people seek to become knowledgeable in medicine ways, and they show their respect by bringing the teacher gifts of tobacco and money. If you ask to learn the ways of a medicine person, he might agree to teach you what you need to do: how long to fast or what songs go with certain herbs, tree bark, and other plants. You would learn the plants for each illness and how to identify them in all four seasons—how they appear, where they grow. You would learn many songs, some of which go with certain plants, and some that refer to an animal or to a bird or to other things. It is a long process, kind of a natural medical school. It takes years, and you don't just learn the medicine itself. You learn how to treat the whole person and the whole situation and how to have respect.

Respect for our teachers means we must be confident when we use medicine. We trust its effectiveness. I never say, "I hope it will work. I hope it will help." The patient places more trust in me and believes in what I am doing when I am sure of the effectiveness of the procedures I am following.

If I come up against something that seems to be so strongly embedded that I can't assure the patient the treatment is going to work positively, I say, "I have some doubts concerning this, and if you would like to find someone else that you feel can help you, you are free to go. Otherwise, if you still want me to try, then that's what I will do and see if we get positive results. It's up to you." If they say, "Go ahead and try it," then I do my very best and call upon not only my power but my constant companion, the bear. Bear Medicine is strength, and not only physical because the bear can project his mind. I don't call upon the bear each time, only in some very difficult situations where I need an extra push. Then I end up asking the Supreme Being to sanction my efforts. He is the one that can do the healing—I acknowledge that at the very end.

In our healing process, we pinpoint the area that needs to be worked on, but at the same time, we consider the person as a whole. We are dealing with a whole life, with feelings and emotions and relationships, such as with a spouse or a child or a friend. Our respect must encompass it all. The people around the person being treated want good for him, and we try to see that it comes about by doing our very best. When we do that, the part that needs healing is taken care of.

We also try to have a clear mind and remain as simple as possible. If we can keep easy accessibility to the particular situation we have been called to assist with, we don't want to cause a logjam. We don't clutter up everything with worries about all kinds of things that could come up. We focus on the help that is needed and our own belief system and hold to our confidence how this has worked for others, and we have no doubt about how it will benefit this person. We stay on that level throughout the treatment. Many times, it takes four treatments to alleviate the pain. We could do one treatment, but the problem might come back the next day, so we do it four times, and that takes care of it. That's what I do.

How effective we are is not our responsibility. Ours is to use what we know and apply it with trust and respect. We are given a sacred trust when we are trying to alleviate a person's problems. With sacredness, respect, and trust, we believe in the efficacy of what we're doing to help, and we do it with confidence all the way through.

We live in a world where there is so much need, and there are many different ways that people have to help others. We should never look down on other people because they don't think the same way we do. We're not in competition with anyone else to help others feel better. We are grateful that we are part of the complete whole of all life, and we are grateful to be able to be of service. We do what we do with a strong sense of humility because we know we are not the ones who do the healing. We are only the instruments through which healing comes.

Whether it's my people, people from other tribes, or non-Indians, one of the first things I have to do before treatment is determine what they're thinking about. Maybe a patient believes that the situation they've asked me to help was purposefully cast on them by someone. I have to dispel that. I might say, "Let's be quiet a moment." Then I can gain rapport, learn what they seem to be thinking about, what they fear they're up against.

Then I'll speak. I'll break the silence and say, "Now, let's talk about some of your dreams. What have you been dreaming about lately?" Maybe some of their dreams relate to what they're asking for help with. People don't know that we dream every time we sleep. We don't remember every dream, so we say, "I didn't dream last night." That's wrong. We always dream; we just don't remember. We remember our dreams if they are significant enough, and there are many, many kinds. Often, I can tell a lot about the nature of an illness by listening to dreams. Before any treatment, the diagnostic approach takes much of my time, as I'm trying to determine which direction will be most helpful.

My teacher often knew who was coming to him for what physical problem before he got there. When they arrived, he'd say, "I knew you were coming, and you were going to tell me about this, so I went ahead and fixed this medicine for you. It's all ready to go now. This is how you take it." He taught me how to gain rapport, even over a long distance, and how to send certain energies long distance as well. I usually use the color purple for sending energies long distance. The color purple is a healing color for us. When you look across the land, the horizon is purplish. That's why, when we send energy over long distances, we use the color purple.

There is a toothache song, but I hate to use it for helping a child because I have to use a little bit of tobacco with it. I blow on the tobacco and sing, and then they have to keep it between the gum and the cheek, right next to the painful tooth, and I have to provide them with something to expectorate in. A child might accidentally swallow the juice and might get sick from it. With a child, I usually just blow on the outside of the cheek and use another song.

I have good success treating earaches in children. I attended the World Shamanistic Conference in Auerbach, Austria, several years ago. There were about 2,000 people registered there, even a gypsy who played the violin. If I was eating near him, he'd come to my table and play.

My room was about two floors above the bar that stayed open all night. Sometime after midnight, someone knocked on the door. I answered it, and it was the barkeeper. He said, "There's a couple downstairs who has a daughter who needs help. She's been to three specialists, but she is still in pain. They were very good German doctors, but they couldn't do anything for her." I got dressed and went down and saw the girl, about 12 years old, and she was crying. You couldn't even touch her ear because it was so painful.

I said, "Okay, stay real still." I performed my chant and blew four times across her ear, and then I repeated it all three more times. Before the fourth time, the pain had already gone away.

Sometimes a child becomes restless, and there seems to be discord in the family—the family is out of harmony. One approach is to burn cedar and sing a little song. I blow on the cedar to fix the bad feelings that some spirit is bringing in so that they may be dispelled. Sometimes a child begins to cry without any physical pain and becomes drowsy but can't sleep. If it's because one of the parents is being unfaithful, we have a particular medicine and song for that. After we use the medicine and the song, we wash the child's face to help them come out of that feeling. The last time I did, it was in Oklahoma City. The grandmother was holding the child to be washed. As soon as we got through washing the child's face, he went right off to sleep.

How a human being develops is important. Humans are affected by their environment, especially by the people around them, as they move through the different stages of childhood. The ways in which they are disciplined have a big effect on them. Perhaps they receive punishments that are abusive, not only physically but verbally as well. We have to be careful not to judge them from the yardstick of maturity, not to criticize a child that hasn't experienced certain things yet. We have to learn to observe them with love.

There are many, many factors that result in the kind of behaviors our children demonstrate. I'm trying to maintain a close relationship with my great-grandson, Ambrose. He's going to need guidance about holding onto things. He will need a lot of help learning to cope with rejection. I see the way he holds his hands like fists at all times. He wants to hold on. When he loses whatever he's holding onto, he's going to lose control.

Sickness in people is not always the problem; a house can be under a spell and cause turmoil. To break the spell upon a household, I have to treat the house, usually at midnight. The song for that is long, and I have to face east and sing it four times. I have a bucket and my blowpipe, and after singing the fourth time, I blow into the blowpipe four times. First, I blow to the left, then to the right, then four times into the bucket, which has water and my medicines in there. After I get through, I go outside and sprinkle the doorway with the water and medicine. Then I go to the right and sprinkle toward the house, all the way around, and then I take a few steps away from the house and sprinkle outward from the house all the way around. Then I go inside and sprinkle throughout every room, including the closets and clothing.

Along with the water in the bucket, there is a wasp nest and some sprigs of cedar. The outside line I sprinkle around the house is so the wasps will warn people that come with animosity in their hearts not to cross the line. If the people come across anyway, the line I put toward the house is for the Little People. The cedar is what the Little People use for their weapons. They warn the people not to keep coming, but if they ignore them and come on in anyway, they shoot them, and their lives are cut short.

That's how powerful it is. The Little People are not doing the killing. The people who are killed have been warned twice. They do it to themselves, so no one needs to feel guilty for the result. You start fixing the medicine right at midnight, and it takes a long time.

For my medicine, it's important for me to be aware of the difference between male and female energy, and how they affect each other: male needs female energy to strengthen its medicine, and vice versa. Whenever I embrace a female, we're exchanging energies for both of us. I don't just take energy and leave the other person weak. If it's a female that is especially in tune with these forces, it really helps me along.

My Tribe and the Seminoles, who now live in Florida, used to be one group. When the two groups broke apart, there were two main medicine men. One left with the Seminoles, and one stayed with us. The one who stayed with us kept the male energy, the energy of the male horn of the rattlesnake, and the Seminoles took the female energy. They are both powerful energies, but when they work together, boy, the power is really there! A medicine woman needs male power, just as a medicine man needs female power.

A medicine woman usually becomes strongest after her menopause because she cannot doctor during her period. The period was designed as a cleansing of the body along the same path that a woman conceives, the path children take to come into the world. To us, a woman's period is very sacred and very strong, a time when powerful cleansing energy goes into the ground. If a man touches or is with a woman in some way during her period, he can temporarily lose the efficacy of his medicine. Every new moon, I fix an emetic for myself because I might have sat next to a woman in her period when I traveled. I fast before I take the medicine, then I go over all my songs to help me remember them. I do it four times to regain the power of my medicine.

Medicine people don't charge fees like doctors; their medicine is given to them by the Creator as a gift to share. Instead, people give to medicine people according to the situation. People used to give blankets, groceries, or other things, depending on the type of illness you were called upon to help. With some illnesses, you might have to stay all night or several nights and maybe do four treatments. Perhaps a hog was given, or if the problem was really serious and you had to stay there several days, a team of horses might have been offered. Nowadays, the gift is usually money. You don't set the amount—the people know how to give.

Before treatment, a non-Indian usually presents tobacco to ask for help. There are several ways you can present tobacco as a token of respect for an elder or for a medicine person. Basically, before you give the tobacco, you say, "I brought this tobacco to give you and ask you to help me," and then you present it. The tobacco is only to honor and request help. It is not a payment for services. When patients give me payment, what they are doing is respecting my medicine ways, which came from above. Many of our elders would meditate alone and receive a song they could use to treat a particular type of illness. We are keepers and dispensers of sacred knowledge concerning illness. That's all we are. I never set a price because I'm not the one that is doing the healing.

There is only one healer. We can bring a person to a point where healing can happen, and then He takes over. That's what we call medicine. There is only one source for healing, and that's the Supreme Being. Whatever we do, we must do it with complete confidence that it will help. If we doubt it, we doubt the power of the Supreme Being. There is no adversary or disease that can stop His power. With that in mind, whatever we prescribe, we must do it with confidence. Our sense of confidence will transmit to the person, and they will go along with a positive response. At least forty percent of healing in itself is just thinking positive.

When my son died in the Philippines, an old friend named Raymond invited my family and me to visit him. He said, "I'm going to share my oldest son, Bubbie, with you. You can call him son. He can call you dad." That's the way it was, and Bubbie became my son. He knew my songs and used the drums when I was singing. On Father's Day, he'd always send me a card. Every time he saw me, and we shook hands, there was a little money he gave me. He was that kind of a son to me.

One night, three boys jumped Bubbie from behind and killed him. They stabbed him and left him dead in the street. After Bubbie was murdered, my nephew got some spring water and took it to the place where Bubbie had fallen and sprinkled it to make those boys who did it give themselves up. That's what that spring water did. He just sprinkled it all around where they had stabbed Bubbie in the back with a knife, and they couldn't help themselves. They gave themselves up.

I was able to see and talk to each of them when they were in jail.

I told them I have every reason to hate all of you because Bubbie was my adopted son. I said to those boys, "I have some medicine power that I could fix and do all of you harm. But if I did that, I would be no better than you were when you did that to Bubbie. I can't do that. Certain power was entrusted to me, and I have to use it in a good way. So, I want to shake hands with each of you and tell you that I'm going to be praying for you."

That's my way. In order for my medicine to work, I have to respect everyone, and I have to do everything in a good manner. I could use my medicine to harm those boys, but I wouldn't be able to help anybody else. The morality of the thing is I can't use my medicine to cause harm, and in my own heart and mind, I wouldn't do it anyway.

CHAPTER 9

LEAVING ROOM FOR WONDER

There's a man I had been praying for whose son died from an overdose of heroin. For several nights I spent quite a bit of time sending my energies to him and his loved ones in order to support them in their great loss. I knew he was wondering why it had happened, and I told him that it's beyond our hands and to honor the choice his son had made in life. He went on to the other side because he had an addiction, and he was not totally responsible for not making the right choice because of the addiction. That's what addiction is all about; we don't have choices anymore.

It took quite a bit out of me, sending energy long distance like that. I have to work with myself because a lot of people call on me for many different things to help with different situations. They don't realize that it's not only them but that there are many others also asking me for help, and I have to spread myself out to cover them all. When others ask for my help, they know I am here.

Most of my elders are gone now, so when I need help, I have to go directly to the One that understands all things. I have to put all my situations before Him. Very seldom do I pray for me. I pray for others—for hope and enlightenment. When it comes to me, my heart's full of gratitude for all the blessings in my life.

I am glad of any support because just the process of carrying life makes a human body tired. I think, sometimes, "If only I didn't have to do this—there are so many things." Sometimes I want to turn my back and go off and just do nothing. But I would not be happy if I did that because this is the path I'm supposed to be on. The Creator will know when I need a rest from all this. So, I just stop for a while and regain my strength by being in the present. By that alone, just being in the present, in the joy and the peace, I'm not so tired. I'm ready to meet the challenges that come when I spend some time in the present, in the now.

If there's a bombardment of things that are difficult, like when we had to move from our home, I go with the process of making plusses out of the minuses of life. That's the way I pray about those kinds of things, and that's how things work out. When they said, "We will not renew your lease," for instance, they were talking to every one of us, including my great-grandson Ambrose, an innocent baby. When I prayed, I said:

"We'll make it some way. My home is not my concern. My concern is that my loved ones, especially the little baby, can have a place. You know your feelings when You gave Your own son to us. No one had room for Him, and they went to a stable where the four-leggeds shared their space. That's where He was born. I know that you have certain plans for Ambrose. You instilled within him certain gifts. Some of them he might be able to uncover and be able to fulfill the good things that You have given him so he can make a place for himself in his life."

After praying, we found our house, and after that, I put tobacco down and prayed again. The next morning, we were accepted, and I said thank you.

I studied with two medicine men from my tribe for 14 years in order to learn my Creek medicine. Before the medicine was given to me, I had to be tested. I had to walk barefoot through a den of rattlesnakes while singing a certain song. One of my teachers took me down into a river at midnight and gave me a white stone to swallow. Before he left me there facing upstream, he said, "If you get scared and go away, it's going to be okay, but that's all you're going to learn."

After he went away, things started coming up out of the water toward me. There was a cow with four horns and little bells that came right at me, then went by. A big snake came at me, tongue out and wiggling, and then went on. I stayed put. That white stone, I guess, was made so I could stand there. If my will was to swim away, I could have done it. But I stayed.

This isn't the way I teach others—I don't put them through trials like that. Right now, though, I don't have anyone studying Creek medicine with me. I have an adopted daughter who lives in Michigan who knows a lot of my songs for different ailments and how to prepare what medicine to use. I don't know whether she'll ever use it or not.

My grandson Bobby, the oldest of my grandchildren, is in line for my Creek medicine, but I don't think he wants to go in that direction. I have passed on a few things to him, including my Christianity. I was there when he and his mother and one of his sisters were all baptized at Rio Rancho Baptist Church. I sang "Amazing Grace" in my own language while they were being baptized.

Because my medicine is in a lot of areas, I pass on pieces of my ways to different people, depending on who can use it. I have shared my fireplace as a Roadman in the Native American Church, my manner of doing sweat lodges, conducting vision quests, and some of my Creek medicine. I give different aspects of my medicine to different people who I think will use it properly. Reginah, of course, has learned many of my ways.

Even though they don't look the same, the pieces of my medicine all have something basic in common. In every one of those areas, we pray to the same God. It's all spirituality. Everything is related to God, everything that we do. That's how I live.

Bear Heart teaching as he holds his Eagle feather fan.
Photograph by Minisa Crumbo.

SECTION IV
SPIRIT

CHAPTER 10

THE VASTNESS OF SPIRIT

I grew up with a Christian mother, a traditional father, and traditional relatives, many of whom were medicine men and medicine women. From a combination of my Christian and traditional upbringings and my studies of other religions, I developed my own understanding of how life can be lived through belief, faith, and trust and by surrendering to the Higher Power. My faith has led me far beyond denominational boundaries into the spirituality that is the basis of all faiths.

Long before churches and the Bible were introduced to Native Americans, we practiced our faith based on our knowledge of spirituality. When we make a Medicine Wheel, for example, a tradition we have had for thousands of years, the first object that goes in is the buffalo skull. This represents the Creator. God is first in all things, and that is why the representation of God is brought in first in the making of the Medicine Wheel. As individuals, we can attain the best of our endeavors no matter what our spiritual orientation as long as we put Him first in our lives.

The four directions are then laid out. The directions of East, West, North, and South encompass the whole world. This reminds us that wherever we go, we take with us the presence of the Spirit and honor the power of God within us.

The Sky is one of our symbols for the Spirit. Wherever you go on this planet, there is always the Sky, and in the same way, the Spirit is always there. Like the Sky, you cannot surround the Spirit; it's much too large. All you can do is experience the presence of the Spirit by opening up your heart and mind. You have to open up and allow the Spirit to come in.

It's all a matter of practice, a matter of faith and trust on the part of the individual. To the extent that we have surrendered to this Higher Being, we experience what love really is. And with love comes forgiveness, so that even though my own flesh and blood suffered on the Trail of Tears, I can look out on the descendants of the people that forced our people to move, with love and forgiveness in my heart, and I can say sincerely, "I love them all."

So many times, the various religions of the world base their teachings on their boundaries. The boundaries make us feel hemmed in—they deny us the freedom to truly enjoy what we believe. We are afraid to overstep the boundaries because we are taught that there are terrible consequences. But when Christianity, for instance, is presented in a loving, open-hearted way, we can live in the freedom of our faith and our trust, without spiritual boundaries. That's why, as a Christian, I have never denounced other practices or religions in my life. Living a spiritual life, no matter what the practice or religion, offers freedom, joy, happiness, and confidence that everything is within our freedom to enjoy it.

FRIEND

— Lisa Costlow —

I first met Bear Heart in the late 80s, when Pat Embers invited him to Manhattan, Kansas, for a weekend workshop. We were a community of spiritual seekers, and many of us had been involved with other gatherings with Native Americans, but Bear Heart took us on our first Vision Quest and invited us to participate in a Native American church ceremony for his granddaughter. Over the years, he solidified the bond among us in that community and helped us expand our consciousness into our relationship with our Divine Mother. He also adopted my son, Dan, as his grandson.

Decades later, in 2005, I moved to Albuquerque to attend the Ayurvedic Institute. Ayurveda is the study of "the Science of Life" according to the Vedas, which are ancient East Indian Hindu texts. I spent many a weekend helping Reginah with the household chores, especially when Bear Heart's health began to fail. It was a very spiritually rich time for me, being immersed in the Native culture in New Mexico and the East Indian Culture, and I will treasure the experience forever.

While at the Institute, I learned how to perform Homa, the Fire Ceremony, and Bear Heart thoroughly enjoyed it when I would do the fire ceremony at their home. On one occasion, he told me he would like to meet an East Indian teacher/pundit, so I arranged to have one of my teachers come to the house. Although the communication was difficult, they greatly enjoyed each other's company and energy.

I was privileged to be there when Bear Heart passed and as we honored him and laid him to rest at his home in Okemah, Oklahoma. Reginah told me he called me "friend," and sometimes, he walks with me in my dreams.

❦ ❦ ❦

Sometimes the Spirit of Christianity becomes lost in the distractions of sin, hell, and fiery brimstone, which would scare anyone. We should not become Christians or members of any other religion because we are scared. We should accept our faith because we believe in everlasting happiness and because we want to experience the peace that passes all understanding in our lives.

How do we put more Spirit in our lives? We don't just go out and grab spirituality and stuff it into ourselves; we must diminish ourselves into the Spirit. That means we give up self-importance and diminish our egos. When Christians are baptized and become members of a church of a certain denomination, they receive the everlasting God. The God they receive is available to everybody all over the globe. It's what the Christians call the Holy Spirit. When we diminish ourselves and allow the Spirit to guide and direct us, help us in decision-making, and point the way that we should go, it's the same Spirit that is available to all people through all faiths.

Our Native traditions stress the importance of diminishing and emptying ourselves to make room for the Spirit. We often fast to empty ourselves of the things that we normally take into our bodies and to provide a time to make a connection with the Creator. He gave us the potential within each of us, our talents to attain certain things, so in all things that we do, it is important to acknowledge that all things come from on high. Our teachings are that we shouldn't take credit for our successes because we know they happened because He allowed it. He has answered us in a positive way, and that gives us more inspiration to live in the spirit of humility, love, and trust.

Sometimes we focus on the ceremonies and rituals of our religious practices rather than what they mean. We forget that they must always be carried out with a sense of humility and acknowledgment of a higher power and wisdom. We shouldn't do them to get a pat on the back or to take credit for this or that. If it's a pipe ceremony, for instance, we shouldn't be proud of the kind of pipe we have, its carvings and decorations. For some, being able to perform the pipe ceremony is a feather in their cap. When they do it that way, though, something always goes wrong; maybe the pipe goes out, or something else happens. It's a lesson for the person who's thinking of self-interest more than what the ceremony represents.

A question we all should ask ourselves is, "How real is God to me personally?" Do we understand that the Creator is a part of ourselves because we are part of all of creation? When we do, we become a loving presence that sends forth vibes that others can feel. It helps us know that God doesn't play favorites. God doesn't accept a prayer from one person and ignore the prayer of another.

Imagine, for instance, that we have a loved one near death. Many families and friends pray for our loved ones, but the loved one dies. At the same time, there's someone of a different religion that's dying. There are other people praying for that person and their loved one's lives. One gets healed, and the other does not. How do we respond? Does it mean that the other group is more favored than we are?

Here is an opportunity for our faith and trust not to slacken. Can we bring ourselves to go beyond what has happened? Perhaps both groups prayed, "Let Thy will be done," and the Creator acted in accordance with His will in two different ways. We experienced days and nights of deep anguish over the loss of our loved ones. It could be that He has allowed us to experience something of suffering so that we, in turn, can help others in the same situation keep their faith.

The challenge presented to the people who prayed for the one who died is that their prayers were answered, but perhaps not in the way that they expected. When we expect answers to our prayers to come in a certain way, it's like putting our wishes ahead of the will of God, rather than truly trusting and asking that His will be done.

True prayer is a complete surrender to His wisdom. When we

surrender and let the source of our lives run through us, we hold in our hands the spirit of great love. We let that strength flow through us. The basis of true prayer is, "Let Thy will be done."

COMMUNITY SPIRIT

— Pat Embers —

Manhattan, Kansas, is just a dot on the map, a small university city surrounded by rural towns, country homes, and farms. We tend to live close to the earth here. Some of us try many things on our land and in our homes to help restore Mother Earth—and ourselves—and we have shared and progressed with each other over the years. We were ready for good medicine to come our way when Grandfather Bear Heart arrived in Manhattan on July 11, 1999.

Over 75 Kansans welcomed Bear Heart and stayed for his weekend workshop held at a local community building. On Sunday and Monday, over half of them participated in Bear Heart's sweat lodges at the Blue Heron Llama Farm in the surrounding Flint Hills. Willow cutting, sweat lodge construction, and fire keeping were done in Bear Heart's way. We worked spontaneously in the woods, at the pond, and at each other's homes with food, prayer ties, and ceremonial objects.

Throughout it all, Bear Heart stressed the importance of community and us gathering here, sharing ceremonies that we have continued to do over the years. He spoke to our hearts and told us he felt at home as he prayed for life and healing, reminding us that healing is "80% our ability to receive and 20% the medicine person's role in bringing Spirit into our lives. Spirit can only bring true healing to those who are ready to accept it. To know and care for ourselves and All Our Relations is our purpose here on Mother Earth."

Vision quests were held that helped us better know our spiritual selves. Our community bonds were strengthened as we realized how much we wanted to share this journey with each other. Bear Heart returned many times after that first weekend.

Things have not all been rosy over the years. It has taken patience, hard work, and understanding to move forward together. It has been worth every bit of effort as we became a more harmonious and committed Earth-based community within the context of our various lives.

Bear Heart brought wonderful teachers with him. We were especially grateful for Reginah WaterSpirit, who was with him as a medicine helper and close companion. She has been our dear friend and a great teacher of her Voice Dialogue methods.

Our visions have expanded over the years. Sweat lodges are appearing on other lands in the community. Bear Heart has authorized some of us to lead the Pawnee sweat lodge ceremony and trained one of our elders as a vision quest leader.

Grandfather Bear Heart's love of his family in Albuquerque was ever-present when he visited. When he was here in Kansas, he was near his tribal Muscogee Creek Nation in Oklahoma, and we know how deeply he felt for them. His laughter, spontaneous advice, singing, and drumming were huge gifts to us. Through all his teachings ran the thread that we can get through difficult times if we hold to the truth and work together.

Perhaps the most central trait of Grandfather Bear Heart was his harmonious love for all mankind and all creation. When we set out on our vision quests, he reminded us that even ticks were teachers. They teach us about our attention, and indeed they did! He reached out to people of all races and beliefs, all walks of life. As an elder, he spoke from his heart and told it like it is. He was a genuine storyteller of life's lessons. He opened a path and brought Spirit into our lives. Grandfather Bear Heart, to this day, continues to be a blessing.

❦ ❦ ❦

Bear Heart dances at Sun Bear's Medicine Wheel Gathering in North Carolina, 1992.

CHAPTER II

SUN DANCE

A NEW MEXICO SUN DANCE

— Tim Amsden —

Bear Heart and Reginah stayed with my wife, Lucia, and me at our home in the high mesa country of western New Mexico for four nights in the middle of July 2005, while they attended a Sun Dance in our area. They arrived at our house late one Monday afternoon and would attend the Sun Dance for most of the next four days. Bear Heart, who had Sun Danced eight times during his life, would be an honored elder and grandfather. He would talk to the dancers and provide spiritual support and his medicine when they were needed.

Each morning, if we lingered too much before he and Reginah headed out to the Sun Dance location, Bear Heart didn't say, "It's time to go to the Sun Dance." Instead, he would put on his hat and pick up his stick and start walking down the road, even though the Sun Dance was 30 miles away. When Reginah noticed he was gone, she'd know it was time to leave, get in the car, and pick up Bear Heart wherever he had gotten to, and go on.

People who would not participate directly, such as Lucia and me, were welcome to attend the Sun Dance, so we left the house on Tuesday morning in our own car at 9:30 am, following Bear Heart and Reginah. We followed our friends along the highway and then down a dirt road as they wove among ponderosas and pinions and junipers to where many tents and an occasional small trailer were scattered. We parked our cars and got out and walked past two sweat lodges, by a large fire pit with six bison skulls on the rim, to the Sun Dance circle.

Around the outside of the dance area was a circle of sunshade where supporters, officials, drummers, and singers were located. Just inside the sunshade border was a circle of small upright sticks marking the dance area. At each of the four compass points, there were gaps in the circle of sticks, gates where dancers and others could enter and leave.

At the center was a tree, and we gasped as we saw it. It was an enormous cottonwood that had been cut down with great ceremony the day before, then transported to the site and anchored in the ground. It stood 60 feet tall, straight and smooth except at the top, where branches and green leaves rustled in the hot July wind.

Hanging from near the tree's top were several ropes, their other ends tied loosely to the tree at its base. Long pieces of bright prayer cloth hung down from the high branches, and there was a horizontal bundle of sticks three-quarters of the way to the top. We later learned that the bundle of sticks was made of branches from the tree of the last year's Sun Dance. This was the third year the dance had been held at that place, and it would host one more. Sun Dances occur for four years in one place and then usually move on to somewhere else.

Reginah and Bear Heart went to sit among the elders, and Lucia and I sat with a number of friends. One was Ruby Quail, who had brought four of Bear Heart's granddaughters out to camp to attend the dance.

We had arrived during a break between dances, and the next dance would be the first that would involve piercing. Before the next dance began, a buffalo robe was carried out to the base of the tree and spread on the ground, and four of the ropes hanging from the top of the tree were stretched out, one in each direction, and fastened to stakes.

After a while, the drummers and singers settled around the enormous drum on our right and began the rhythmic thump and repetitive song, which would continue through every dance. The dancers, who had been given a talk by Bear Heart beneath the blue sunshade to our left, entered the circle. There were almost 60 of them, slightly more women than men, and they passed in line through one of the gates, raising their hands and turning. They moved into a shuffling dance in a clockwise circle around the tree. These people would dance for three days, six hours each day beneath the intense July sun, without food or water, until the last dance was complete.

Often a couple of young men would circulate with forked sticks holding a can the size of a large coffee can which contained coals. They would scatter sage on the coals and hold the can out to the dancers or pass it over the base of the tree or the buffalo skulls. They would also move around the circle of observers, and each person would bow their face into the smoke and pull the fragrance of burning sage over their heads. They moved about the area throughout the four days of dancing, a continuous cleansing process.

Four people would be pierced during this dance, and a few would be in each dance thereafter until most or all the dancers had pierced. Piercing for men involved placing two small wooden dowels beneath the skin on either side of the chest. The piercing for women was similar except that it was done on the outside of the upper arms just below the shoulders. The men were laid on the buffalo robe at the base of the tree for their piercing, and the women were pierced while they stood. Then each of the four people who were pierced for this particular dance were led to one of the ropes stretched out to a stake in the ground.

The ropes were removed from the stakes and attached to the dowels, tethering the dancers to the tree. The tethered dancers danced in place, facing the tree with the ropes loosely stretched out and up, while the other dancers continued to circle behind them. Eventually, after a series of movements in toward the tree and back out, the tethered dancers lunged backward against the ropes and broke free.

When dancers tethered to the tree broke free, there was a collective sympathetic sigh from everyone there. When a person who has danced in the hot July sun for hours or days without food or water finally pulls from the rope, you feel with them a great release.

We few scattered witnesses felt privileged. We were there because we were supporting someone who was participating or because we were deeply interested. As we stood for hours watching and rhythmically moving our own feet to the drum, we couldn't help but become a part of the deeply powerful spiritual process going on around us.

Each evening Bear Heart and Reginah returned to our house. Despite the fact that he had been "working" all day, Bear Heart would be full of energy. This was particularly surprising, as Reginah said he spent a good portion of each night keeping her awake by praying softly. At dinner, we would ask Bear Heart questions about the Sun Dance. Here is what he said about why people Sun Dance, and how he addressed the dancers:

> "Why do people dance the Sun Dance? How many human motives are there? Maybe a dancer has a very sick relative or close friend, and they might dance with that person in mind. Maybe they want an answer to a question, like what direction they should go in their life. Perhaps they just want to express their love of Mother Earth. There are as many different reasons for dancing the Sun Dance as there are dancers.
>
> Before I talked to all the dancers, they asked me to sing the

Sun Dance Song that my Lakota brother, Black Elk, had made. That's what I sang, and then I went on. This is what I told them. I said I appreciate your participation and the time you took to come here and make the sacrifices and to bring whatever it is that you have in your hearts and minds.

I said that I am an eight-year Sun Dance man. I've been through the same things you are going through now. At some point, to test you, the elders will sit and drink water and eat watermelon in front of you. Last year, I was among the elders who did that, partly because I had to go through it when I was a dancer. To be able to withstand temptations like that in order to fulfill your vow develops your inner being and helps you to become stronger within yourself. Not only that, but it will help you emotionally to appreciate all of your sacrifice and expressions of love for the life that's been given to you.

Whether you are representing your family or just yourself, I know how important it is for you to be here and take part. All of our activity together can be expressed in one word, "spirituality." That's what brings us together and makes us brothers and sisters of all cultural backgrounds, all colors of skin. We're here for a common purpose.

So, I send my blessings to each of you dancers, and especially to those of you that are going to give up your blood and let Mother Earth absorb it. I want you to have a lot of courage and confidence—that's what you must have if you're willing to do this. It's not an easy thing, but it's very, very worthwhile.

Before the European influence of religion, our teaching was that in order to be blessed in a good way, you have to suffer. The first teaching of Buddhism is that all life is a struggle. We appreciate and acknowledge the life that is a gift to us and say thank you to the Creator for giving us another day.

Our Mother Earth is very old, but she still gives to us—things we wear, things we eat, things we live in, things we drive. In our very small way, when some of our people shed their blood, it rejuvenates the life of our Mother. It's a way of saying thank you, acknowledging that she is a real mother to us and all things."

CHAPTER 12
VISION QUESTS

Native Americans have gone on vision quests for hundreds of years. Originally it was done for the safety of the tribes—young warriors or tribal leaders would go out for several days without food or water to commune with the Great Presence. They were seeking strength and guidance in a world where battles with other tribes were common and when the presence of deer and buffalo couldn't be counted upon.

Today, vision quests are used mainly to find direction in our lives. They usually last up to four days and may involve many questers who go out at the same time, each to a different solitary spot. People often find a personal power symbol on their quest, like an animal or plant, and afterward may be given a name by the quest leader. In a vision quest, you don't eat or drink. No food or water. When you are fasting, you empty yourself so you can receive something from above—something to motivate you, inspire you, guide you in a way that you should go. That's the purpose of a vision quest.

When I first get to the vision quest gathering spot in the morning, I put down an offering of tobacco. The fire that will burn throughout the quest has been started, the rocks for the first sweat are heating, and the questers go out to find their individual places. As they are looking, I pray for permission to use the areas the questers will use.

Often the spots are under the charge of some particular bird or animal. Through my prayers, I tell them that we're going to take up some of their space, but we're not going to destroy anything. I tell them that when they see my people out there, they're there for a certain reason, and the people won't harm them or their place in any way. And all around, I ask the birds and animals to hold back. I ask if they come to my people, please do so only to give them certain things that they can use in their lives. I pray like that and put tobacco in the fire. That's just the beginning.

About nine o'clock in the morning, there's a four-door sweat lodge to cleanse and prepare the questers. Because the sweat is for the questers, supporters can fill in only if there's space. I like a single circle, but on occasion, if there are not too many, three or four can sit up in front of the others. I tell them about what they are going to do and give them some general instructions. I also tell them not to accidentally spill the drinking water that is being passed around, or it will rain.

After the sweat is over and they get dried off and their clothes on, I meet with them one at a time. I talk to them about what the quest can be for them. I ask them to think about these questions: who am I, why am I here, what are my gifts, what am I supposed to be doing? I never let them promise to stay out all four days or two days or anything like that because they might have to come back early. A person doesn't have to stay out for a particular amount of time for their vision quest to be successful and significant.

After I send everybody out, I put tobacco down on the ashes and the coals all around the fire. I form the ashes into a snake shape and say, "You snakes are our little brothers. If you see some of our people in your area, please, don't go near them. Go your own way. They're not there to harm you. I ask you, please be gentle and don't try to harm them in any way." This is a blessing for the snakes, in addition to a prayer for protection. In bear country, I make the ashes into a bear. The fire burns day and night while they're out on their quests.

The last part of April is when the snakes come out of hibernation. I once sent my adopted daughter-in-law, Sandra, out on a quest, and she picked a spot close to a rattlesnake den. When she saw the snakes, she said, "My father will take care of this," and they never bothered her.

I have a map that shows where each person is. Throughout the night, at ten o'clock, midnight, two o'clock, and four o'clock, I smoke a pipe for each one out there. I pray on the Milky Way. It is the Star Nation, which is made up of those who have gone on. I ask them to watch over the people; I pray that they'll be safe and have good communication from on high, and meet the things there that will be helpful to them. I pray for each one of them four times during the night.

I don't go out physically and check on them. If one of the questers needs to see me, they tell someone. That way, I can keep my concentration on all those I send out, and I don't get it all mixed up. Maybe there's one quester from 20 years ago still out there, but I don't think so.

When everybody comes back in, they have a one-door sweat. I meet with each individual to help them understand what they experienced. Each quester will have a different experience and see different things. They see a butterfly over and over in a place that isn't the habitat of butterflies; it's telling them something. The butterfly wasn't always a butterfly. It was a caterpillar first, so its message to the quester may be about transformation. If they see a squirrel, we may talk about how they prepare for winter by storing up the nuts they're going to need. It's a great blessing if they see a spider. Most creatures have to go way out to hunt, but a spider doesn't have to leave its home. It weaves a web and what it needs comes to it.

Snakes are powerful messengers on vision quests. In order for snakes to survive without legs or arms, they have to be wise. Ancient Egyptian rulers made snake amulets and placed them on their foreheads to give themselves wisdom. We call snakes our little brothers, and we're not afraid of them. Even though I'm not actually out there with them, a part of me, perhaps something I said while we were in the sweat lodge, or while I was talking to them, or praying for them before I sent them out, will come to their minds. That's the way it can work with the quester.

When you send people out on a vision quest, you're making it possible for them to be close to the Creator. I keep a prayer in my mind asking the Creator to send down a vision: a new concept they hadn't thought of before concerning their lives, the direction they should go, and how they should go about getting there.

Vision quests can change people's lives. Sometimes people realize they were not specially chosen to follow the path they have made for themselves, that there is an alternative path that would be more beneficial to them, a more pleasant career than the one they are following. Often, we follow a certain direction in our lives because we are not fully aware of many of the things that go along with it.

When someone finds during a vision quest that they need to change the whole direction of their lives, I stress a positive attitude rather than a negative, to help them focus on the new. We don't throw the negative out the window, though, because it's very helpful. How would we know what is positive for us if we didn't have the negative to compare it with? We honor the presence of the negative, and it enables us to become more positive.

WORDS FROM ANOTHER VISION QUEST LEADER

— Mike Andrews —

I give people three words before they go out because there can be a lot of fear. There's fear of night, there's the fear they're not going to get a vision, and there's general performance anxiety. The three words I like to tell people are surrender, empty, and nothing. Together it's a seven-syllable mantra, and it's also a koan. Surrender doesn't mean giving up; it means relinquishing control. Empty is what you need to be in order to be filled. Nothing is what we aspire to, a way to enlightenment.

The hardest parts of guiding vision quests are interpreting visions and naming. You have to know what to focus on. The first thing that people talk about after their quest is important, but also important is the thing that's the most loving. A major part of the process of giving their vision quest name to questers is love.

I went on a vision quest, and there were eight golden eagles circling. When I talked to Bear Heart after the quest, I wanted him to give me the name "Eight Eagles," but when I described my experience, I said, "I saw eight eagles." The name I received was "Eagle Eye."

When I wanted to go in there and talk to Bear Heart and quickly get the name "Eight Eagles," it was ego, and I finally convinced myself that Bear Heart knows better than I do. The name incorporated my vision as an artist, and I love that, and I surrendered—that's the bottom line, to surrender. For Bear Heart, naming and helping people deal with their vision are the primary elements. It's not how you send them out or how you do a sweat lodge; those are just details.

At one quest, we had a guy who was out for four days, and when he came back, he said, "The woodpecker did this, he went up a tree, he did this, he did that." He was trying to say that his name should be something about a woodpecker. Bear Heart said, "Don't worry about your name. I'll name you. I'll tell you about your name." The name that Bear Heart gave him was "Learns to Live in the Moment." It's not a very positive name but think about what this man can learn when he says, "My name is "Learns to Live in the Moment." That's what makes a loving vision quest name. It's not just what they want to be named, but what can be of use to them. Whether they're named after a woodpecker or an ant or something else, it's hard to get just the right name. You have to think, "How can I help this person?"

❦ ❦ ❦

Instruments for Native American Church ceremonies.
Illustration by Bear Heart.

CHAPTER 13

NATIVE AMERICAN CHURCH

There are many different ways that people pray to the Creator. The ways don't matter because it's always the same Creator. Sometimes the ways get blended together, but the Creator doesn't change. The Native American Church is like that.

In 1861, there was a nine-year-old white girl in Texas named Cynthia Parker, who was captured in a raid by Comanches. She was taken into the Tribe, where she grew up and became a member, both in her mind and in the way the Tribe treated her. After a while, she became the wife of a war chief and had three children. One of her children was Quanah Parker, who became chief of the entire Comanche Nation, and created the Native American Church.

At some point, Quanah was gored by a bull, the wound became infected, and he was cured by a Mexican curandera with peyote. He had converted to the Methodist faith and read and studied the Bible and found that he liked the teachings it contained. He liked the church to which he belonged, but he also loved the teachings and the motifs of his people, such as the tipi, and believed that peyote was a sacred herb. He gathered together his Bible, his Native American paraphernalia like the gourd and the drum, and some dried peyote buttons and peyote tea. He took these with him and went out and fasted for several days and nights.

When he got hungry, he ate peyote, and when he got thirsty, he drank peyote tea. He prayed, read the Bible, sang, and meditated. When he finally returned, he got his people together and told them, "I have found a way for our people to help themselves through prayer and the use of peyote as a sacrament." He was, of course, familiar with the Christian sacrament of communion that uses grape juice or wine to represent the blood of Christ.

Quanah told them that he saw many things from the Native way of life as symbols of what he had read in the Bible, such as how the open flaps of the tipi represented open arms to everyone with a sincere heart. This was the beginning of what came to be called the Native American Church. Peyote could provide answers to most anything, but peyote was not worshipped. It was acknowledged as a gift from the Creator that was put on the Earth to help the people.

As Quanah and his people gathered together, they began to sing songs. The songs came to them as they ate peyote. All of the songs have a tendency to acknowledge how pitiful we are as a people, how we've been deprived of our lands and our hunting grounds, and how, with the buffalo diminished, we can no longer survive by hunting.

The people had pipes, but they were awkward to use in meetings, so several people went out and fasted and prayed, and they came to the conclusion that cornhusks with tobacco should be substituted for the pipe. We use these for our prayer smokes. When we pray, the smoke takes our prayers up to God.

In the Native American Church, the bow and arrow were replaced with a long stick that represents the staff Moses used for the salvation of his people when they crossed the Red Sea. We say that as long as you hold this stick and hold your belief system, you can rely upon the salvation this church promises, salvation through Christ.

TO BEAR HEART

— Steven MUQIT Sachs —

Fancy Dancer, Medicine Man,
Peyote Road Man!
We perceived through your eye
With the Four Winds of seeing;
Fearlessly working with the introspection
Of the Bear, to reclaim
Our unnamed but true Self
As an essential part
For the transformation of our world.

🪶 🪶 🪶

There's a roadman who is the person who conducts the ceremony; a drummer; a cedar man; a fireman; and someone, usually a woman, who brings in water in the early morning. The fireman sits at the doorway so he can take care of the fire outside all night long. As the drummer drums and the singer sings, one person uses the rattle, holds the staff, and sings four songs. Then they pass the staff and the rattle on to the next singer, and so it goes all the way around, all night long. People who don't know the songs or don't want to sing just pass the rattle and staff to the next person. There are many, many other things that happen in the ceremony, but what I'm trying to point out is that the church is based on the teachings from the Bible.

As word got out about the church, the settlers began to complain. Anything that went wrong was blamed on those people eating that "loco stuff," going crazy, and doing all kinds of wild things. So, the government sent historians, ethnologists, anthropologists, and anyone else they could think of to investigate. One of those was a historian and ethnologist named James Mooney. He was permitted to attend some of the meetings, and he told the people, "You have something good here. There is the danger that the government or missionaries of different denominations might try to come to stamp this out. So, in order to protect yourselves, you should charter this as a church." Because of his suggestion, on October 5, 1918, a group of leaders met at the house of my Cheyenne uncle, Mac Haig, near El Reno, Oklahoma, and made up the charter of the Native American Church, which was then filed with the government.

Peyote was used long before the Native American Church was chartered; the Mayans gave it to their long-distance messenger runners so they could keep up their stamina. Native people also used peyote for clairvoyance, for such things as trying to locate missing horses—did some other tribe steal them, were they camped nearby? This is how peyote became part of a church ceremony. It was due to Quanah Parker being converted to Christianity and then having his vision of how Christianity and his Native practices could be blended while he was out fasting and praying.

During a Native American Church ceremony, we eat peyote and drink peyote tea. We use green peyote if we have it, but if not, we use dried peyote. It doesn't matter how much you eat. It's your faith in God, faith that he put these things down here for our benefit, that counts.

Peyote was first analyzed in 1938 at Princeton University, and they found that it contained nine alkaloids. Since that time, they've identified dozens more. Sometimes if people are sick, they pray to direct the peyote to their ailment. Many people have been cured in one night, in a Native American Church meeting.

The place where they get peyote today is kind of barren like Golgotha, where Christ was crucified. It is in the southern part of Texas near the Mexican border, and they call it Peyote Gardens. When we think of a garden, we imagine a place that is lush green, but Peyote Gardens isn't like that; it's full of cacti and weeds and rattlesnakes. That's where peyote is found.

A roadman, the one who conducts a Native American Church ceremony, has to be authorized. I was authorized as a roadman by an adopted father, Joe Carson. He was an Otoe from Redrock, Oklahoma, and a great medicine man. He authorized me to use his ways, and those are what I use whenever I conduct an all-night meeting in a tipi or sweat lodge.

There are many wonderful stories about Joe Carson, especially about his great sense of humor. One time after a meeting, before everyone left the sweat lodge in the morning, he pointed to a man, got his attention, and, using sign language, said, "You and I have been friends a long time." After the man nodded and acknowledged it, Joe signaled again. "Way before these others started coming in here, you and I were friends." The man nodded again. And then Joe said, "By the way, what's your name?" They'd been friends a long time, but Joe Carson pretended he didn't even know his name! That's the kind of man that he was.

During a ceremony, the people sit in a circle, and in the center is an altar. The altar is made from dirt or sand and shaped like a crescent moon, with a line all the way around it. The line is the road of life you want to follow. You've got to move carefully because the road is really thin; you could fall off. That's the road the roadman is named after. He's not called a roadman because he goes on the road.

In the middle of the crescent moon altar, the roadman puts a piece of peyote called the chief peyote. We don't pray to the peyote; it's a focal point for God. We pray to God through the peyote and smoke our corn shuck with tobacco rolled in it as we pray. The smoke carries our prayers up toward heaven, to the Creator. When we are through praying, we put the tobacco out and put it on the altar.

Sometimes you hear about the red road, and that means something else. The red road is the Indian way of living in the good medicine way. There are two medicine roads: red and black. Someone wanting to follow an evil medicine way uses the black. The red road is good medicine, and that's what I do. But the red road isn't necessarily the same as the road in the Native American Church.

Mostly, there are not Native American Church buildings. The ceremonies are traditionally conducted in tipis, but they can occur anywhere they are needed. In one place in Wisconsin, they have a permanent building with a permanent altar. They teach young boys how to conduct the meetings, and they perform baptisms. The State of Wisconsin officially recognizes it as a church and accepts the baptisms of its members.

Since it was chartered, the Native American Church has endured many assaults from other organizations, religions, and denominations. Some people believe that the adherents of the church are pagans who worship idols. Those who speak like this have never been inside; they have never experienced what goes on in the church. Yet, in return, members of the church turn the other cheek and pray for those who are protesting against them. And the church is still going strong, from Oklahoma to New Mexico, in Arizona, up north into the Dakotas, and in Kansas.

We know that we have no power to develop the Spirit; it's already perfect. The human is always trying to become perfect, but Spirit is perfection within itself. In order to contain more of it, we have to yield more of ourselves to the Spirit. Instead of developing the Spirit, we experience the wholeness of it by letting the Spirit lead us in all things, by willingly surrendering.

Wherever we go, we should go with awareness of the Spirit and practice the power of the Creator within us in all of our endeavors. As individuals, we can attain the best of our endeavors no matter what our spiritual orientation, as long as we put Him first in our lives. One thing we have in common with other religious beliefs is that we know we were all created by the same Being. We know the Spirit abides within all of us.

BEAR HEART AS ROADMAN

— Bob Bergman —

I knew Marcellus for 36 or 37 years. I met him when he was about 50 years old, and he was always someone with a lot of dignity and presence, someone people always recognized as a wise person who should be listened to. We attended the same Native American Church meetings in Navajo country. We would frequently drive from Gallup, New Mexico, to wherever the meeting was going to be. On various occasions when we wanted Marcellus to run a meeting, I'd go get him in Oklahoma City and then fly him back to Gallup, and after the meeting, fly him home to Oklahoma again.

Years and years ago, he was one of the mainstays of quite a large area of Navajo Native American Church people, all over the south-central part of the reservation and around the Gallup area. Marcellus trained quite a few Navajo roadmen to whom he's given his fireplace, as they say. He was very influential with a great many people, not only in the immediate ceremonial matters that he taught but also life in general.

If you are a roadman who authorizes someone else to be a road-man, it's called giving him your fireplace. You don't literally give him a fireplace; you give him your way. My brother Tommy, for example, was given a fireplace by Jack Coshoway, who was an Otoe who came to the Wide Ruins area and lived there a long time as sort of a missionary in the Native American Church. He gave Tommy his fireplace, but Richard, my other brother, got his from Marcellus.

Different roadmen run different kinds of meetings. I think that one dimension on which meetings vary is how much talk there is about emotional issues. Marcellus was very good at sensing the important issues, and he moved into them in a way that got other people to speak. He knew the things that people were worried about and spoke to them. I remember a meeting where there were only a few people, and Marcellus sensed that some were concerned about the low attendance. He told us all that the empty places were good because they were filled by those who had already gone on.

I didn't experience this, but the woman I was then married to said that during the course of one night, there were a number of young men who were there, and in the morning, they were gone. Through one thing and another, it was clear to her that they were the spirits of people who had recently been killed in the Vietnam War that was going on at the time. Marcellus originally spoke about it because he sensed that people were worried.

As I think back, his way of being a roadman was like his way of doing anything. He was clear and eloquent so that any time it was his turn to speak, he offered something that was particularly well said to the point and moving, with a lot of layers to it.

Marcellus was good in the Indian way of giving advice without giving advice. He was not likely to say, "Do this, do that," but he'd tell a story that would have the appropriate moral. He led Native American Church meetings like he lived, full of love and caring for everyone, no exceptions.

Several years ago, we had a Gourd Dance in Lawton, Oklahoma. The President of the Navajo tribe, Peter MacDonald, was there, with a clan relation who was being inducted into the Gourd Dance Society. I was also being inducted. Peter MacDonald was in school where I was field representative, and I was best man at his first wedding, so we were very close.

I was introduced to Peter's clan relation, Dooley Shorty, and later saw him dancing the Gourd Dance without a gourd. I happened to have an extra one, so when that particular round was over, I went to him and said, "I saw you gourd dancing and saw that you didn't have a gourd, so to make things right, I'm going to give you a gourd to dance with. Then you can say you are gourd dancing." That was the beginning of a long relationship. Dooley eventually became my adopted older brother.

Dooley had a contagious laugh, and when he laughed, everybody laughed. He had a real nice attitude about people. One time Reginah and I gave him a ride, and we wanted to eat somewhere before we took him home. Along the way, Reginah missed a turn, and we went far out of our way and had to turn around and come back. When we finally got to the place we were going to eat, Dooley said, "Good driver, just missed the road." We always remember that. Every now and then, if we get lost, I tell Reginah, "Good driver, just missed the road," and we remember Dooley.

Dooley was a Code Talker, one of the Navajos that volunteered during World War II. They were partly responsible for the war turning in our favor because the Japanese could not break the code when they talked in Navajo, a very difficult language. An important thing to consider is that at that particular time, the Indians of Arizona and New Mexico were not allowed to vote. Yet, they still volunteered to serve because they loved the land they called home, the land where their loved ones were buried, where their families lived, and they grew up. They were ready to defend their country in order to prevent the war from being fought over here in the United States. Despite their right to mixed feelings and emotions, they made great contributions to preserving this country, and they are now celebrated for their important part in winning the war.

Dooley and I both became roadmen in the Native American Church. The fireplace he used was a Comanche fireplace that my Otoe uncle had received from friends of his among the Comanche tribe, and my uncle had authorized Dooley to conduct the service in his way.

When his second wife died, Dooley didn't go to meetings anymore, so I started taking him to meetings with me. In those I was conducting, I would have him sit next to me and use the cedar for me. I wanted him to get as close as he could to that peyote we put on the altar—we call it Chief Peyote. I wanted him to be real close to it.

I suspected very strongly that the meetings were difficult for him because a lot of memories were coming through. The meetings go the entire night, and early in the morning, a woman, often the roadman's wife, brings the water in. She sits across the altar from the roadman and joins in the prayers. I know that he used to sit at the same place where I was sitting, facing his wife as they prayed together. I knew he missed that.

I would pray for him and pray that he might find strength and, in time, take up as a roadman again. I hoped that maybe his daughters or granddaughters could pray with him as his wife had. That time finally did come, but not right away. Things had to work out through many prayers before he prayed as a roadman again.

I began traveling out of the country a great deal, so we didn't get to see each other as often as we used to. Dooley met a Winnebago man trained in Lakota medicine ways, who became an adopted father and took him to different places for ceremonies. That's when he decided to conduct Native American meetings again. Then he had a grandchild for whom he wanted to pray on the grandchild's birthday. But just before that took place, Dooley Shorty died from a heart attack, and he never got to conduct a ceremony and pray for his grandchild.

Not long after Dooley's death, I was asked to conduct a meeting near Taos, New Mexico, and I wanted to invite Dooley's son. Dooley had other children, but this son used to travel with us when Dooley and I were traveling to meetings together. He would lay down behind us all night in the tipi while the meetings went on. I hoped that in time he might decide to take up the position of conducting meetings

I went by Dooley's home, and one of his daughters was there.

I asked about her brother, and she said he was working downtown in Albuquerque. I asked her to tell him where I would be, and if at all possible, to bring the ceremonial box that Dooley used when he conducted meetings. I wanted to cedar the box off in front of the altar. Also, I had made a Chief Peyote for Dooley, and I wanted to pray with it and put it on the altar all night and make it so that his son could use it for his own family.

I had made the Chief Peyote because Dooley had asked me to, and I used it at his home when there was sickness among his children. He would have a fireplace going when I got there, and we would put cedar down and cedar the Chief Peyote and set it before us, then we'd pray and fan off the ones that were ill. Even though the son hadn't been authorized to conduct a whole meeting, he could use the Chief Peyote the way Dooley and I did when his children were sick.

That evening when I was ready to start the meeting, Dooley's son arrived. I had him sit next to me, and we prayed together all night. That was when I got a chance to pray for Dooley's grandchild. I prayed as his brother to bless the grandchild the way Dooley would have wanted him to be blessed, to grow up healthy and strong, and to have a good life.

We are close to Dooley's daughter, too; she went to school at the Institute of American Indian Arts in Santa Fe. When we adopt each other as brother or sister, father or uncle or aunt, son or daughter, we make this family as real as the family we are born into.

The relationships we make stay with us and come back. Maybe the person that you interacted with and chose to be your relative will inspire you to go forward as they do.

I don't talk about Dooley in the past tense because I'm very certain that a special place was made for him when he was called away into the great beyond. That is the place that all of us will go to at a certain time, but until that time comes, we must do all that we can to try to fulfill the potential that's been given to us here on Earth. These are things we don't know before their time. The relationship that Dooley and I made together as brothers goes on. It is very meaningful to me.

HECTOR GOMEZ PRAYER AND HEALING

— Robert Seidenspinner —

We had known for some time that our friend Hector Gomez, a roadman in the Native American Church, had health problems. In addition to diabetes, he had been diagnosed with Hepatitis C, a virus that deteriorates the liver over time. Hector entered the hospital suddenly with severe internal bleeding. As it turned out, a couple of vessels had ruptured around Hector's liver, which is why he was losing a lot of blood. Upon further examination, it was determined that only ten percent of Hector's liver was functioning. Hector was admitted to the intensive care unit of a local hospital in critical condition.

Shawnina, Hector's wife, rushed to his side from her home in Arizona. Because Hector was virtually in a coma, Shawnina acted as the interface between the family and the medical staff. Once Shawnina realized the seriousness of Hector's health, she immediately called her adopted dad Bear Heart. She asked Bear Heart to conduct an emergency meeting of the Native American Church on behalf of Hector and the family. Bear Heart came out to California from New Mexico within a couple of days, and this is where my story of healing—an example of intention and prayer facilitated by Bear Heart—begins.

When Bear Heart arrived from New Mexico, he went immediately to the hospital to see Hector, who was semi-conscious and still in critical condition. Bear Heart prayed at the hospital, mostly for Hector to be able to move into surrender and trust and not be in fear, which under the circumstances was huge. He prayed for Hector as he lay on life support with all types of tubes connected to his body and his life literally hanging by a string. I was there at the time and watched closely all that was going on. The apprehension in the air was thick, not only around Hector but also from the many family members and friends that filled the hospital. Here was a man who had conducted many prayer ceremonies when called upon by others in need, and now Hector needed prayer, and that need did not go unanswered. Bear Heart shared with me that there was not much he could do at the time except address the fear of the unknown that he felt in the hospital room and then conduct the Native American Church ceremony.

It takes a lot of effort and planning to sponsor a Native American Church meeting, but in about three days, all the necessary elements seemed to come together. Everybody pulled together for Hector and his family and prayed for his life that was hanging in the balance. Bear Heart had agreed that he would use Hector's personal Native American Church instruments and box to run the meeting.

The night of the meeting, you could feel the energy crackling. Johnny Hernandez took care of the fire, Calvin Magpie's son took care of the drum, and Bear Heart took charge of the meeting early on in a very focused way. Before we rolled our smokes, he told us that this was a healing meeting, and we were praying for a man's life. Bear Heart let us know that he wanted us to see Hector not as he was at the moment, in the hospital on various levels of life support, but as we knew him in some other way, smiling, laughing, and happy. Bear Heart directed each of us to call up a vision of Hector as healthy, strong, and full of life. As Bear Heart set this tone, something deep inside me knew we were on the correct path, and this was definitely going to be a healing ceremony.

That night we prayed all night long, sang, and ate medicine. The meeting was powerful, and soon after, Hector took a turn for the better. He had a procedure done and came out of the coma. Another big miracle was that he was put on the list of those to receive a transplant, despite the fact that he had no money or medical insurance. In fact, at the time that he was placed on the list, he was not an official citizen of the United States. Hector Gomez had prayer in his life, and it worked for him.

We prayed for his recovery for body, mind, and spirit healing. We prayed for whatever it takes to bring this all about. During the two following meetings, we prayed for the transplant to take place in a way that Hector would not have to be unconscious and in a coma before he would receive it, and that was the way it happened. Many of us attending received healings, whether we were aware of them or not. Bear Heart was healed, as was Calvin Magpie, and the fireman John as we saw him open and felt his heart soften. That's the way American Indian Church meetings work.

❧ ❧ ❧

After my son was killed in the Philippines on May 11, 1964, wearing the uniform of our country, three of my adopted brothers, members of the Otoe Tribe at Red Rock, Oklahoma, came to my home in Oklahoma City. They said that I had helped them and many others when they lost loved ones. To show their appreciation, they wanted to sponsor a Native American Church meeting on my behalf so that I might receive spiritual strength to keep on helping other people. I told them, "Whenever you set the time for that meeting I want to come and take part and show my respect to each one of you."

So that's what we did. In the course of the meeting, I was looking into the fire, and I saw the image of a bird come out of the ashes. The bird was the anhinga, which is a symbol of the Native American Church. The anhinga is a water bird with a long neck and tail feathers like a turkey. Its habitat is southern Florida, where it lives by diving and catching fish. When it is swimming, all you can see is its long neck, which looks like a snake. The Seminoles of Florida call it the Snake Bird.

To me, it was like seeing the eagle of the plains Indians that flies high and carries prayers to the Great Spirit. Seeing that bird gave me a wonderful feeling and let me know that my son was all right. I knew it was his time to go, and I must accept that fact so that when my time comes, I can be reunited with him in the great beyond. Those were my thoughts when I saw the anhinga in the fire.

Four Generations of Bear Heart's family. Photograph
by Reginah WaterSpirit, 2006.

SECTION V
LIVING WELL

CHAPTER 14

BEING

One of the most significant words we have is "beauty," and the greatest beauty is the beauty of love: the loving touch, the loving caress, the loving sentiment, the loving feeling of hope we can transmit to someone who feels depressed. There is a well-known Navajo prayer about beauty—may beauty be on top of you, behind you, in front of you, beside you, and inside of you. May your wholeness be beautiful. That's their approach, to see life and other individuals with love.

When love directs our relationships with people of all creeds and colors, we see them as parts of the complete whole. We feel gratitude and happiness. And that's what most people are always seeking—to be happy.

Many young people today are on the outs with their parents. Rather than appreciating and loving their parents for who they are in their lives, they say, "My parents don't understand me." Love and understanding, though, have to flow both ways.

When I hear a young person say their parents don't understand them, I sometimes ask, "How much time have you spent trying to understand them? Don't you think they have their own wants and worries? Who took care of you when you were ill, fed you, and supported you when you were sad? Don't think only of yourself, as if everything is for you. It's good to honor our parents. Even though they may have died long ago, we still have the opportunity to love and honor them by the way we live." That's something we can all think about.

Love allows us to accept the dualities of night and day, guilt and non-guilt, negative and positive, black and white, man and woman. You can see the beauty between two people who love each other and are together and full of joy. You can almost feel their love in the look they have, the closeness, and the support that runs from one to the other and back. We are made to uphold one another, so we shouldn't touch one another with dirty hands and minds. We should move as much as we can into respect and honor toward each other, upholding the wonderful person that walks beside us. He or she was made by the same Creator that made all life forms. We need each other more than we realize. When we love, we access the strongest force. It's the only force that can open a human heart—not even an atomic bomb can do that.

There are many reasons two people come together. They could be attracted to each other at first because of similar backgrounds, mutual interest in their careers, purely physical reasons, or other things. Whatever brings them together at the beginning, they need to keep their hearts open, accepting, and full of love if their relationship is to survive.

Along with love, we also need to have forgiveness. Most people can't do that. We were given not only a brain but emotions based on love that asks us to overlook the mistakes of others, never point a finger of scorn at anyone anytime, for any reason. If we're going to point, we should point to ourselves first. We forget that we've done the same thing we're judging others for many times or thought of it. We're not as goody-goody as we sometimes think we are.

Before we judge others, we should recognize our own shortcomings and forgive ourselves. If we can't forgive ourselves, how can we forgive anyone else? So, these are just a few of the things that need to be considered in order to keep love in a relationship.

Some people are stubborn, some are closed-minded, and sometimes there should be parting for the good of both. When two people are not compatible, not only physically but also in their personalities and mindsets, they should separate. I've counseled a lot of couples, and I often talk to them about the word "responsibility." I tell them it means developing the ability to respond in a thoughtful and loving way. It means beginning to understand one another's point of view and accepting those things. If one person thinks that what they want or believe is the way it's going to be and won't budge from it, the relationship becomes one-sided and has little chance of success. If both feel that way, they cannot possibly make it work.

With couples, so many things are involved. If they have children, it's especially complex. Who do the children identify with when there's conflict? What happens to the children if they part? These are thoughts that I have about my own grandchildren. All of them live with their mother, and their fathers live elsewhere. When I look at my grandchildren, I sometimes wonder where I failed my own children. Did it start with my daughter after my son died?

After my son's death, it was a long time before we started eating at home because my wife used to talk to my son after school after she came home from work. They'd sit there in the kitchen and talk while she was fixing dinner. After his death, she couldn't stand to be in that kitchen anymore.

Finally, I had to say that we had to live for this one that's left with us, our small daughter. And so we began eating at home again. I have asked forgiveness for my neglect, for not dealing earlier with things that I knew were going wrong. Mostly, I am working on forgiving myself. Losing a son like that was a big lesson to me, and I am still learning from it after all these years.

It helps me to remember that one of the greatest gifts given to all mankind is the freedom to choose. When we exercise this freedom with trust, it helps us endure any situation. The painful things in life contain great value if we don't just look at their surface but look inside. When we understand that we were put here for a reason, we can pursue ways to fulfill the purpose of our own lives so that they coincide with the will of the Creator.

The mind is great with its intelligence and knowledge, but knowledge is nothing unless you know how to use it. That's where wisdom comes in. We can use the mind for specific tasks but shouldn't become identified with it. Wisdom resides in our hearts. Life was actually made to be fairly simple, but we make it complicated and end up in confusion. We need to lighten up. We have to be patient with ourselves as we learn these lessons. I'm still working on it. Patience is central to our teaching—when an elder is teaching a younger person certain things, the younger one wants to learn right away. He or she must learn to be patient. That's what our elders teach: to be patient, to wait for the right time.

The father of two of my grandchildren has gallstones and kidney stones. We know that someone who has kidney stones likes to be in control of all things. My daughter is a Scorpio, and she also likes to be in control, and that's why they are no longer married. If we are observant, little clues such as these come together into pictures that help us understand why things happen as they do, especially if we can use plain observation without judgment. That's how things appear and reveal themselves. All of us would benefit from working harder to develop observation without judgment. In fact, a non-judgmental approach would improve all areas of our lives. A strongly judgmental nature, especially when it's combined with a lack of acceptance of things, leads to an excess of anger, and anger is detrimental to health.

I originally came to New Mexico to be an associate in the field of psychiatry at the invitation of a psychiatrist friend. My friend had a good practice and a beautiful home, but his home was taken away by the government, and he failed a test he needed for his psychiatric practice. Those two incidents, losing his home and failing the test, filled him with such anger that he developed two tumors in his brain. Surgeons removed one tumor, but the other one was larger and in a place where it could not be operated on, so he died from that second tumor in his brain. The doctors said he died from a brain tumor, but he really was killed by anger.

BEAR HEART REMEMBERED

— Walter Dominguez —

I first met Bear Heart in 1982, when I heard about a gathering of Native spiritual elders to be held in the mountains of San Diego County in California. I was in my 30s, and though I had met the love of my life, Shelley, and married her, and had an excellent education and exceptional opportunities to advance a career in filmmaking, I was at a crossroads in my life. I felt stuck, confused, and spiritually empty. I sorely needed guidance and inspiration.

Something impelled me to pack my camping gear in the car, kiss Shelley goodbye, and drive to what was called a Medicine Wheel Gathering, which had been organized by Sun Bear, a Native leader, and by a collective of seekers called the Bear Tribe. For an entire weekend, I heard a number of traditional Native elders speak and lead ceremonies, including sweat lodge ceremonies, and I was greatly moved by their wisdom and kindness.

When Bear Heart spoke, I was instantly enthralled by both the man and what he shared. Like many great spiritual speakers, he could shift your emotions from levity and laughter to suddenly opening your heart and bringing tears to your eyes. But for me, what made him stand out was his kindness, approachability, and great sense of humor and laughter.

At this gathering, I also met some young men and women who were similarly pulled to this event and to Bear Heart. Those people became spiritual relatives to me in the following decades and remained so to this day. And some of these relatives, like Miguel Rivera and Glenn Schiffman, having the long mentorship and support of Bear Heart, eventually became spiritual teachers and leaders in their own right.

Upon returning to Los Angeles, some disturbing things happened that made several of my new friends reach out to Bear Heart and urgently ask him to come to visit us. He heard our plea for help, and he came as soon as possible. He ran a sweat for us and used his healing skills to make special medicine to protect us, especially the children. He told us that whatever negativity was being sent our way would have to go through him first. We all felt comforted and more secure through his caring attention.

We didn't realize it then, but we were quickly evolving into a spiritual community. For my wife Shelley and me, along with the others, this was the start of decades of profound spiritual practices and experiences with Bear Heart. He opened the door for us to the beautiful Native traditions of sweat lodges, pipe ceremonies, vision fasts, tipi meetings, and other profoundly empowering and healing rites.

Looking back, I marvel at how all our lives wonderfully changed course so quickly and dramatically. One way or another, we were all at a crossroads when we met Bear Heart, who was like a brilliant comet that swept into our lives and took us all with him on a whole new trajectory—a great and fulfilling spiritual adventure.

Bear Heart always said that the fundamental problem with Western education is that we are taught the skills needed to make a living, follow ambitions, and make money. But we are never taught how to live. There is no thought given to how to become a balanced, loving, responsible human being. There is no teaching about how to properly relate to your family, friends, lovers, life partners, and others. No instructions are given on how to live in harmony with our fellow human, other life forms, and the Divine Spirit that is the source of everything. And so, Bear Heart devoted himself to teaching us the missing and very important instructions on how to be a human being.

Bear Heart became a frequent guest in our home, and we became very close, which in itself gave us rich memories and teachings to cherish. He gave us the opportunity and responsibility to conduct ceremonies and healing rituals that have been a treasure trove of satisfaction and joy, a way to be in service to others while helping us to become more fully dimensional, our true selves. Among these memorable rituals was a marriage ceremony conducted within a ceremonial circle, as well as another ceremonial space where a young couple was able to mourn the baby they lost in the most beautiful and profound way imaginable.

One of the happiest memories Shelley and I had together with Bear Heart was when we sponsored an adoption ceremony that he led. The people we adopted became our spiritual sons, daughters, brothers, and sisters, and our relationships continue full of love and care. Above all, we adopted Bear Heart as our spiritual father, and he adopted us as his son and daughter. This was one of the highlights of our lives, and even now, long after he passed and after my wife recently passed, I have often felt his fatherly presence with me, implanting in my thoughts new ways of looking at things and imparting his love and support.

There is one more teaching Bear Heart gave me that has held me in good stead. It has kept me from wasting my time and from needlessly disturbing my emotions and mental equilibrium. He taught me that when we give a gift to someone, we should unconditionally relinquish it, release it without fixating on whether it is valued or used. The gift can be an actual thing, or it can be something intangible: an opinion, advice, a sharing from our hearts, or simply loving care.

Deciding that when I give something, I will also relinquish it has been one of the most important of Bear Heart's "how to live" teachings for me. It has saved me from a lot of hurt feelings, and it has taught me to be more judicious in what I give or share—so it's only what I can honestly fully release, with no strings attached.

The teachings Bear Heart shared have brought greater peace to my mind and soul and helped me become a better and more fulfilled man. He made possible a more loving and rewarding marriage with my wife and gave us a spiritual community of brothers and sisters to which he has provided continuing love, nurturing, and support. He left us all with tools that allow us to live good lives without fear of death. Marcellus "Bear Heart" Williams was a brilliant and wonderful light for me and so many others, and his light just keeps shining on.

🌿 🌿 🌿

Sometimes we make bad choices. Instead of twiddling our thumbs and regretting, we should see that there are valuable lessons there. We should honor our mistakes because we learn from them. Our mistakes become our teachers; they teach us to not make the same mistake over and over again. That doesn't mean we don't always look for improvement. As soon as a building is completed, it begins deteriorating. While it is here, we should make the best use of it, just as while we are here, we should make the best use of our lives. There is always somebody who can do some things better than we can. What is expected of us is to do the very best we can in the areas we have chosen for ourselves.

Be true to yourself and do not think that you need to be what others want you to be. Stop looking around and trying to meet the expectations of others. Look within yourself and accept the fact that this is who you are. We have many sub-personalities that take over sometimes, such as anger, depression, and guilt. In order to cope with those things, it is important to honor them and say, "You've been teaching me things I did not understand, but now I do. Thank you." Speak to each one of them this way. For example, "Anger, you sure have put me through a lot! I've slammed doors and kicked things! That's the bad side that helped me see the good side. I was too blind to really appreciate the good on the other side. I want to learn this great lesson. Every time I feel anger coming through, I will use it to appreciate the positive."

It's also good to try to operate within the present. Use past experiences for things learned, but don't dwell there. Come forward into the now. That's going to best prepare you to meet the future. We don't disregard the past or the future; they exist for a reason. The past is full of learning, and it got us where we are. The future is where possibilities lay, the place of potential. But live in the present.

When we dwell in the present, our sense of awareness is high. In the stillness of the present, we begin to sense our deeper self. We disassociate from the chattering mind, the constant dialogue that goes on inside of us all the time, "Yak, yak, yak!"

Our minds are important tools, but they are not who we are. We should learn how to use our minds when it's appropriate and then lay them aside. Once we can begin to still our minds in the present, we go deeper. We find a sense of peace that we perhaps have not felt in a long time.

As we become better at remaining in the present, we begin to shed stress. We stop focusing on our feelings that maybe things in our lives did not come out well. As we begin to be in the now of our lives, we discover peace that is beyond words: a sense of joy, of being. This is where we find the happiness that people are searching for.

We think if we take care of this, take care of that, eliminate this, merge into that, and acquire this, we will be happy. Yet it never happens because all that compulsiveness alienates us from our true selves and from being. The closer we get to being, the more we know the answer to the question, "Who am I?" We can answer, "I am."

There's so much joy that most people fail to experience. They may feel happiness now and then, but it's short-lived. But once you live in the present, in true being, there is no limit to happiness. It's not something outside that you get by doing; it's in the quiet present within you.

When you're in the present, you can deal better with pain. Sometimes when I have pain in my body, I laugh it away, saying, "Joy, thank you for coming, my attention is here in the present. I'm going to rely upon my deeper self, and I'm going to enjoy." As I begin to laugh, the pain weakens. The more pain there is, the more I laugh, and eventually, that pain goes away. It doesn't take knowledge of healing processes to know this. It's just living in the moment.

There's a lot of pain in the moment of giving birth to a child, but there's a lot of joy too, because of the life that's coming into the world. It's how we use pain that matters. If we accept it, don't try to fight it, there's no victory for the things that oppose us. The pain doesn't make us kneel down and say, "I give up." It goes away.

Spending time in the now allows us to sense creation through the balance and harmony that comes into our lives. At the center of everything, there is an intelligence so great that we can't begin to conceive of it with our small minds.

In a workshop one time, I told the story about a young boy that asked his dad if they could go see the parade one Saturday in their small town. The father agreed, and they went and stood on the street to wait for the parade. Finally, the parade started, and people rushed forward and stood ahead of them. They couldn't see, so the father picked the boy up and put him on his shoulders so he could see the parade going by. The boy said, "Oh, there's a clown! Oh, there's this, and, oh, there's that. Oh, Dad, I wish you could see this!" He did not know that when his father was small, his father sat on the shoulders of his own father so he could see a parade.

This story is about all of us, whoever we are and whatever we're doing, because there have always been those who let us sit on their shoulders. Maybe it was a teacher, a minister, our mother, or some other relative. But for each of us, there were many, many who have helped us along the way so that we can be where we are now.

Then I said to the people in the workshop, "You come up here and relate some significant time in your life when someone helped you at the moment when you most needed it." And man, some voices broke down when they recalled certain times. It became a wonderful thing.

Once you get into the practice of being thankful, it's good to also think about the support you get from the earth and from all of nature that surrounds you. You will find yourself walking with respect for what supports you, breathing in the atmosphere that sustains your life. See how the trees stand as our tall brothers, and the sky as our tipi covers us. The birds, the leaves rustling, the grass swaying, everything is joyful. Be grateful that we can be surrounded by such joy—even from nature.

When you are with other people, do you bring joy? Do you bring a sense of closeness, or do you drive people further away? Those are some of the things to keep in mind and to keep us on the path—to have gratitude for being able to be of service to others and to extend love wherever we go. Like Johnny Appleseed, who sowed seeds of apple trees wherever he went, we can throw out seeds of love to the hearts around us, even to the four-leggeds, to all life forms, but especially to our fellow human beings. They need not know who we are or what we have done. We don't do it for that. If we could instill in others that same sense that we feel, that brings us so much joy. If we can pass that along, that's what really matters. We're not here to get a pat on the back.

There is an old saying in our Tribe that if you only read or hear about something, you don't know it; you only know about it. After you yourself experience that particular kind of situation, then you can say you know it. The best way to teach anyone anything is to let them experience it.

People say "teach me" without realizing that patience is what most of us need. If we can learn to be patient and live in trust and acceptance, we will learn what we really need to know from the examples and experiences that are set forth before us.

We also need to understand how to bring more responsibility into our lives. We have many responsibilities, but our first and greatest responsibility is to ourselves. Responsibility comes from learning how best to respond to the circumstances and situations that come before us. Do we just react, or do we gently respond in a compassionate way? Do we approach situations with a view of how they could be meaningful to both ourselves and the other person?

If we live by certain guidelines, we must be careful about sharing those guidelines with others. We should ask ourselves if our guidelines fit into the other person's belief systems. We should consider whether they might lead to something that can benefit the other person, not only in a material way, but help them achieve the very best in what they have chosen to do in their lives. These are the kinds of things they don't teach us in brick schoolhouses; we have to learn them in other places.

Schooling is not confined to a four-walled classroom. Blackboards are everywhere. Many of the teachings of my people come from nature. Bears, for instance, are noted for their insight. Their eyesight is not real good, but they make up for this with intuitive powers. They are very protective of their cubs, especially the mothers. They catch fish to survive. Their little cubs are awkward when they first try to fish, but their parents don't punish them for it. Instead, the parents make a game of fishing. They splash water on the cubs, and the cubs splash back. Even though they are struggling for survival, they make a game of it—what a lesson for mainstream society.

Many people are bored by their jobs. Monday morning comes, and they have to force themselves to go to work. Do they look at the many who are unemployed? Are they thankful that they have employment? Are they always looking for promotions and envying people in other situations, or do they do the very best they can in the present? If we thought more often about those who are struggling just to survive, we would find more gratitude and joy in our own abundance.

When I was young, one of my elders said, "Do you see that tree over there?" I said, "Yes." He said, "If that tree could talk, it could teach us a lot of things." He told me to put my legs and arms around the tree and then to observe without judgment.

I learned that the tree is a lot like us. It has long roots with which it gets nourishment from our Mother Earth. It nurses from our Mother, who sustains the life of the tree. Its life-sustaining sap is like the blood going up and down in our own bodies. The sap goes up the trunk to the big branches and into little branches and out to the leaves. We say, "When the wind blows through a tree, the leaves are singing praises to the Creator." In late fall, the sap stops running. The nutrients that used to go into every leaf on the tree come to a standstill, and the leaves begin to fade, but when you see an autumn tree from a distance, it's a very beautiful sight.

What does this mean for our own lives? When we near the end of our lives, are they beautiful like the tree? As the leaf becomes a nutri-ent for other life forms, will we leave something behind that will be beneficial to those that come after us? I learned a lot from that tree.

I guess the majority of people are afraid of snakes. The Kickapoos in Texas use snakes rather than dogs for guards. They're very friendly to the snakes. They allow the snakes to come into their area, giving them the food that they like, just like they do with any other living thing.

In my Tribe, we were always told that snakes are our little broth-ers, so we should never be afraid of them. We learned that if you are really afraid, you will attract their attention. The proper thing to do is to honor them. That's what we do. We are taught to be around and accept all of nature as we find it. There are a lot of lessons to be learned from the birds, from the trees, from those that crawl on the land and live in the waters. They have much to teach us.

Sometimes we are in such a hurry that we don't take the time to appreciate the lessons nature has for us. That's when we should slow down into the harmony of the moment. Our people say, "Look at the tree and how its leaves wave in the breeze. They don't go against one another as the breeze moves them. They move in accord with each other and with the direction of the wind. They're in harmony."

Being a warrior is an individual effort, but being a part of an army of warriors requires teamwork. We should keep focused on our common causes. If there was a flood and people are together throw-ing sandbags on a levee, they don't stop and ask each other, "Hey, what culture do you represent? What's your belief system?" Everybody pitches in for the common cause.

Don't fantasize about the way you wish the world could be. Accept nature as it presents itself. It is the way it is supposed to be. You will then be able to go more easily from nature into the spiritual because spirit is the state of perfection. It is something we cannot truly define, something we just accept.

A young woman came to me, wanting to know how to expand her intuition. I told her that what she needs to do is to meditate on her own. She should become relaxed and ask that illumination of her best direction come forth when the time is right. She should then think of nothing and allow the desire registered in her unconscious to work. She might find the answer in her mind at the end of her meditation, or it might come to her later when a particular situation or state of mind calls it up. It will come to her when the time is right.

Often when I'm asked to speak to a group, I have no idea what I'm going to say. If I'm centered in the moment, the right words just come from within. Things I've heard, read about, or experienced come into my mind, and I intuitively know how to present them. That's how it can work for this woman. Her true desires in life are already known by her unconscious. In order to access that knowledge and the abilities she wants to develop, she needs to relax, especially relax her mind. It takes practice, but she will be at her greatest strength when she is totally relaxed because that's when she is receptive to power that's within her. She doesn't have to go through a lot of dramatic things. It's very simple. There may be complicated rituals that also work, but they're not as powerful as a simpler approach.

Everyone is born with intuition—all they have to do is to become aware of it and develop it. Many psychics have foreknowledge of things that happen, but they don't understand it at first. Sometimes being able to foretell events starts at a very young age. You don't have to be special for this to happen— we are all psychic.

We have both a conscious and an unconscious mind. Just like the conscious mind, the unconscious has intelligence and receives experiences. When we live quietly in the moment, we access the unconscious mind, allow it to give us guidance and information. Our intuition works more powerfully when we acknowledge that it comes from beyond the power of the human level.

We know a lot of things about the physical makeup of the ethereal and logical sides of the brain, the old brain that our people depended upon in the beginning, and neurotransmitters. We have uncovered many things, but we still have a lot to learn. Our scientists don't understand intuition at all, and transmitting thoughts to another person over a long distance is a good example. We know it works, but how is it possible? We are just beginning to discover the power of thought. Some people think that in order to send a thought to another person, you have to build up a strong energy and push that thought way out, but that isn't so. Like intuition, you are stronger when you are most relaxed in the present. When you are relaxed, there are no barriers to deal with.

If you want to send a thought to someone else, don't think about the distance. Just concentrate on transmitting a thought to another mind. The person may not be aware that you sent the thought to them, but you know it made it through when they say, "I thought about you out of the blue the other day." Or you might get a letter that says, "All of a sudden, you came to mind." You don't have to respond by saying, "I was sending messages from my mind to your mind." Just say, "I was just thinking about you too."

THE TEST AND THE FEATHER

— Bob Bergman —

I have known Marcellus Bear Heart Williams for many years and could tell stories about him for hours. One of my favorite stories about Marcellus happened when I was taking the American Board of Psychiatry and Neurology oral exam. The first time I took it, I flunked. I was going to take it again, and about a week before, I was in a Native American Church meeting that Marcellus was running. I told Marcellus about the upcoming exam before we went into the meeting.

I described to him how the night before, I had kept seeing a feather, a very specific Eagle feather that fanned me off all by itself. As I thought about the feather, I thought that it had to do with my taking the exam. The following rationalization had occurred to me: Benjamin Rush, whose picture is on the seal of the American Psychiatric Association and was one of its founders, was a signer of the Declaration of Independence, which presumably he signed with a feather. That was what I was thinking about.

Well, sometime during the meeting, after midnight water, Marcellus came around and put some cedar on the fire and fanned me off with the exact same feather that I had been seeing in my mind the night before. He gave it to me as a present, and he said, "This is what you need in order to pass your exam." Then toward morning, he gave me a stern talking to. He said, "When you go and take this oral exam, you have to think about it in the right way. Think about it as though you were going to apply for a loan at the bank. Before you go to apply for a loan at the bank, you put on your good shoes and your good clothes. You call them sir, and you act like you want them to like you, and then they'll give you a loan. Behave like that, and you'll pass the exam." His advice was a nice combination of Marcellus's Indian way and his knowledge of the white way as well.

I saw him recently for the first time in many years, and one of the first things he said to me was, "Do you still have that feather?" My answer, of course, was "Yes."

CHAPTER 15

BEING TOGETHER

With all the various traditions and beliefs there are among different individuals and countries, it's very important that we try to expand our knowledge of how others live. We should study how their values compare to our own and how we could benefit by merging some of our values and ways of doing things with theirs. The more common ground we have, the better are our chances for peace in the world.

We have far to go in terms of learning to communicate in ways that will engender peace among people of different belief systems, cultures, and races. The first step is to accept the fact that the ways and beliefs of every people are just as valid as those of any other.

One of the main causes of war is when one religion or people look down upon others. When belief systems hold that particular people are chosen above others by their god, it justifies fighting and killing those of lesser status. For us to be part of the solution, we need to be sure that our belief system respects the beliefs of others—whether or not we understand exactly what they are.

In our Creek belief system, wherever you stand on this planet is the center, and it's connected to everywhere else. You affect whatever happens throughout the world, and it affects you. We should live in a way that helps those who might follow our example of belief and trust. It is our responsibility. We should never force anyone to try to believe in a certain way. Our job is to live our beliefs, our faith, and our trust in such a way that others might also find their way.

Maybe someday, there will be common denominators that will unite all people, common elements of our belief systems that will allow us to live together in peace. We should strive toward this goal, but we won't be able to get there alone. We have to work together, and we have to appeal to higher knowledge and wisdom to provide ways by which we can unite in mutual respect. We need to put our energies in this direction, not only for ourselves but also especially for those that follow after us.

It is important to wait when we pray. We have to learn how to keep quiet and listen for an answer. Are we too impatient? Maybe we have waited for an answer, but have we really listened for the answer? How many of us really know how to be still, to wait and listen?

In the teachings of Buddha, the first lesson is that all life is a struggle. In order to survive, we have to utilize what has been given to us. We have to know what we're living for. We have important things to do.

Everything and everyone is made for a purpose. Things aren't brought into being haphazardly—they all have lessons for us. Look at the delicate and beautiful butterfly; it teaches us transformation. If we're going to transform, we want to transform into beauty, and the highest form of beauty is love. In order to truly love, we must forgive, and it goes the other way too. To truly forgive, we must love and know ourselves.

Unlike the old days, Native American youth today rarely receive teachings from their elders. They live in the modern world of cell phones, rapid transportation, and television. They often have little or no information about their Native traditions. When they aren't taught these things, they grow up not knowing who they are.

Once when I worked with the Education Department of the State of Oklahoma, I was asked to visit one of the schools to meet with four Native American students who were having difficulties. The school officials wanted to give them one more chance before they were to be expelled.

I got them together and asked, "What's the problem here?" They said, "They don't like us." I asked, "Who do you mean? The students, teachers, who? They don't like you for what?" They said, "All of them because we are Indian." When I asked what tribe they were from—were they Choctaw, Cheyenne, Cherokee, or what, they didn't know. I said:

"I want you to quit this B.S. that they don't like you because you're Indians. You don't even know the names of your people; you can't speak your own languages. You've got to find out who you are and fly right, and this school's an opportunity to begin. Years ago, you might have made it by common labor, but it's harder to do that now. The learning you can get here will start you off to a better life. Get with it! I'm going to check on you."

You can start by not skipping school. When you don't make it in school, what's going to happen? Where will you go? What will you do? Your parents won't always be there for you to bail you out of trouble. Think about these things. Think about it all.

I checked on them every week after that, and they did well. They stayed in school. Our young people need to hear messages like that from their elders, learn how to have pride in themselves. We should tell them that instead of throwing in the towel, they need to use the towel to clean themselves up, clean away their bad thoughts, and let their inner qualities shine through.

Almost all Indigenous people include rites of passage in their practices. Especially important are those used by the community to move boys and girls into adulthood. Before the rites of passage for boys and girls begin, they usually receive teachings. Male elders teach the boys, and woman elders teach the girls. Their teachings focus on the responsibilities of being an adult and how to think and behave like an adult. They touch upon such things as courtesy, respect, and being a person that considers the good of all people.

As the elders talk to the boys and girls, they might stress relationships: the importance of differentiating between infatuation and love, and different ways to properly express love. They might talk about how to choose a good life path and other aspects of living well within the community.

There is a movie called *The Emerald Forest*, in which a tribe of people in Brazil captured a small white boy named Tommy. Tommy was taken into the home of the chief and his wife, and the chief noticed that as he grew older, the boy became interested in a beautiful girl about his own age, and they played together a lot. One day the chief and his wife and some of the elders went out into the forest, where they found the young boy and the young girl playing.

The chief called out, "Tommy, I want you to come here because it is time for you to die." His wife, in the role of motherhood, asked, "Must he really die?" and the chief said, "Yes." He and the elders took the boy out into the forest, stripped him of his clothes, and threw him down on an anthill. The boy writhed as the hungry forest ants covered him and began to bite. He remained on the anthill all night long.

When morning finally came, the men took the boy down to the river and washed off all the ants, and brought him back to the tribe. Then the chief said, "Tommy as a boy has died. In his place, a man has been born." He gave Tommy a drink that caused him to hallucinate, and he soared up in the sky like an eagle and experienced insight into many things before he came back. Later, Tommy was given teachings and chosen to be a warrior. He eventually became a chief, and for each of those changes, there was a rite of passage.

Rites of passage for initiation into similar stages of life have been practiced among most of our Native American Indians and have been passed along from generation to generation. In modern times, however, these practices are almost non-existent, and their value is being lost.

Several years ago, when I was involved in a workshop in Virginia, I gathered all the men together and talked to them. I said, "I'm going to talk to you about an important rite of passage. If you have never been pronounced an adult, you may still be operating on the psychological level of a boy. It's important that you know what it means to be a man and accept and understand not only the responsibilities of an adult, but the many other things that are involved." I talked to them about those things as they sat in the circle, and at the end, I fanned each one of them off and pronounced each an adult.

After I left, I received a number of phone calls and letters telling me how much their lives had changed for the better, especially their work relationships and their relationships at home with their wives and children. Their interactions with all the people around them improved, and they were beginning to live in greater harmony.

Other than Jewish bar and bat mitzvahs and Hispanic quinceañeras, there are few rites of passage today for moving our people from youth into adulthood. I imagine that's one reason why gangs are formed. Young men have no society that welcomes them into adulthood and teaches them what it means. They turn to gangs because that's where they find their rites of passage—affirmations of themselves as adults.

That's also where a lot of other unbalanced lives come from: a wife-beater, a hotshot junior executive who thinks getting ahead is all that matters, a coach that rebukes rather than encourages his players, a psychiatrist who pushes her clients into gray areas of thought. All of these individuals have one thing in common. They become adults without ever really learning the responsibility of true adulthood and what is expected of them. They have never participated in a rite of passage that marks their shift into the adult part of their lives, that formally places the proper responsibilities and privileges into their hands.

I would like to promote the establishment of rites of passage for today, put together and administered by elders of different places and cultures. Because of my age, I have to suggest it for others to create and perform, but I think it would go a long way toward unifying and socializing our people. In time it might help us learn how to live together and better exemplify the first words of the Constitution of the United States, "We the People."

There should be a requirement that the elders who conduct the rites be authorized to do so. They will tell the young people about healthy relationships; choosing a good path; and being responsible members of their family, community, and nation. Their teachings will flow from the wisdom of their years and life experiences. As they conduct one ceremony after another, their skill and understanding will grow. After their teachings, they will perform a ritual marking the passing away of the boys and girls and the arrival in their places of adults.

When we help our young people to properly become adults, we improve our community, and we improve the government. We help them understand their responsibility to do the best they can.

In some ways, the changes that have happened to the leadership of this country over the years are similar to the changes that have happened to the leadership of many of our tribes. Traditionally, the chief was the poorest man in the tribe. He was there to serve all the people, and he did it without resentment. If the men went on a hunt and they brought back game, the chief gave his share to the widows who could not go out. When people lined up to eat, he always stayed in the back and let others eat first—everything he did as chief was based on his sense of duty.

One of our great leaders was Black Elk. His visions were almost like the Book of Revelations in the Bible. Once, he and his people were caught on a knoll, surrounded by enemies. They had no water, no food, and there was no way out. Black Elk had great medicine powers, but he didn't have a chance to work those powers from where he was. They were totally surrounded and did not know what to do.

All of a sudden, the people thought they heard thunder, but the thundering didn't stop. It continued, and they saw it was coming from a cloud of dust. The cloud was made by a huge herd of buffalo that Black Elk had seen in his vision. The herd came thundering around, and the enemies that had surrounded Black Elk and his people had to run away. Because of the intervention of the buffalo, the people were able to survive.

I'm not saying that we should employ such things as Black Elk's vision for leadership of our tribes these days, but Black Elk was true to his beliefs based on his sense of duty to all his people, and that is what made him a great leader. Now we have chairmen who have replaced the chiefs. Many of them have learned dirty politics. Some of them are involved in under-the-table dealings. They get kickbacks for contracts and put their cronies, rather than the best-qualified people, in leadership positions. Perhaps because they have never before handled so much money in their lives, many have wound up in prison.

The value system of the old days is not there anymore. Honesty used to be a very important quality, and our chiefs knew that they had to be honest with themselves before they could be honest with anyone else. They had a strong sense of duty. They knew that things should be done, not just for the good of the ones doing it, but for the good of all the people. They were willing to do and give of themselves without putting their hands out for payment. Those were qualities our leaders tried to live by.

It seems that the leadership of our country has gone the same way. In the old days, when a farmer's barn burned down, the neighbors would have it back up in a few days by contributing their time without holding their hands outstretched for payment. Today, we've lost our focus on the overall good and our concern for all people.

The sense of selfless service isn't there. The belief that the government should help everyone, especially those most in need, has faded. Our money says, "In God We Trust." How many of our leaders read that anymore? Too often, they only read the amount on the bill. Now, money and those who have it come first. Today, the leaders are the first to eat.

This country has been in war after war over the years. The War of Independence, the War of 1812, the Civil War, World War I, World War II, Korea, Vietnam, and the wars in Iraq and Afghanistan, are major pieces of our history. Many of those wars were right and important for this country and the world. But the world is quickly changing; we are all much more connected.

Technology allows us to instantly see and talk to almost anyone anywhere on the globe. Our environment is suffering worldwide damage, and commerce involves every country. Also, the ability to wage devastating war has become widespread. All of this means we've got to improve our ability to get along and live together as one-world people, building something good for those that come after us. We've got to ask, what are we going to leave behind? And the question has to be asked not just in the United States but by the leaders of all governments.

Mankind has used violence to settle disputes since the beginning of time. In the Bible, there was the first murder by Cain of Abel, and a God who unleashed his vengeance upon groups that warred against his people. Because God was thought of as a god of vengeance, a different viewpoint was needed, and God sent his Son to interpret Him as the God of love. Somehow, we have forgotten all that; we are unwilling to put it into practice in our lives. If someone slaps us, we don't turn the other cheek; we retaliate, as our government is doing at this moment. We do not draw upon God's ways and negotiate for the good of all people.

The ones who did such terrible things on 9/11 were an extremist group attacking what they saw as evil that was represented by the World Trade Center and the Pentagon. They thought they were doing something right in the name of their God, Allah, to destroy evil. When they attacked the Pentagon and destroyed both towers, they thought they were doing something godly.

Rather than trying to understand their viewpoint and come up with a response that took it into consideration, we immediately retaliated, first in Afghanistan, then by attacking Iraq. Our attitude seemed to be that you can't fool around with a big power like the US.

Maybe if we had taken some time to understand why the attacks in this country happened, if we had gone back to our spiritual roots, we would have had a more measured response. We might still have attacked our enemies, but hopefully, we wouldn't be where we are now, losing young people's lives and the respect of the world. Where does prayer come in? Where does respect for others come in?

Our greatest focus should be on negotiation with all countries, especially those countries like North Korea, that don't like us. The spirit of our Constitution is respect for the rights and thinking of other people. Instead of always retaliating, can't we look at what causes others in the world to criticize us? Can't we look at ourselves more closely so we can negotiate better understandings, better relationships, especially with those that don't like us?

Documents can be beautifully written and have great meaning, but they're only words on paper. They mean nothing unless we translate those words into deeds. The words of the Constitution are much like the words of the code of the Iroquois Confederacy. The code of the Iroquois Confederacy was created long before the US won its independence and became a vessel for peace for the five great Native nations that agreed to its words.

We should go back and look at the Constitution of the United States. It's a wonderful document. It begins with "We the People," but do we stand together as a people? Can the teachings in our schools present our ideals in such a way that students will learn that they are a part of a great nation and an entire world? We should ask for the Creator's guidance to help us stand together as one people, grateful to live in America as citizens of the world.

During my first trip to Washington, DC, I had a chance to meet with President Harry Truman. I was given just a few minutes in the Oval Office with him, but he kept me longer. I was a Baptist minister, he was a Baptist, and we prayed together.

As we talked about many things, I noticed all the papers on his desk. I realized that when he signs his name on those papers, he's not just signing for himself, but for all the citizens of the country. He's signing them for me.

I prayed for him, not only for the man but also for the office that he represents. I prayed that he guides the country properly and well for all the people. I prayed that he be given wisdom and help as he made decisions. I would have prayed this way, whether I agreed with him or not.

We should all pray for our presidents and other leaders, asking that they receive the guidance they need to lead the country. Those people need help to work out solutions for the good of the country as a whole. I think many people fail to pray for our leaders because they don't think the country is going in the right direction, but that's when our prayers are most needed. If we can stand together spiritually, we can do many wonderful things under the spirit on which this nation was born.

One thing our leaders should not lose is their sense of humor. Often you see people in high positions, and you don't know whether they even know how to smile. My people teach that those who can't laugh at themselves can't understand others. They say that a person without humor always has a chip on his shoulder, and that means there must be wood higher up.

The Bible tells the story of the disciples arguing about who's going to sit on the right side of Jesus, and then Jesus walked into the room. I can envision the glint of humor in his eyes as he tells them to be sure they get into the kingdom before they start arguing where they're going to sit.

People sometimes tell me that I live an interesting, extraordinary life. I do feel blessed, and I am grateful to all my teachers for the work and struggles they went through to share their gifts. I know, however, that when we look with open hearts, we see that each of us has an extraordinary life. We all have the same opportunity to be of service every day, especially when we understand that when we interact with any living thing, including humans, it is sacred.

A long time ago, I was in a coffee shop with an elder. He pointed to a man sitting by himself at a small table in the back. He said, "You see that man sitting over there? He doesn't know anything about our traditions. He's an old man. When he dies, what will he have passed on that's going to be helpful? I'm telling you this—I don't want you to just become an old man. Learn something useful, something to leave behind to benefit others."

Portrait of Bear Heart at 80 years old, 1998.

SECTION VI
GOING ON

CHAPTER 16

BEAR HEART PASSES

— Reginah WaterSpirit —

The last week of Bear Heart's life was a struggle. It felt like he wanted to pass on but was having a hard time. I thought that I should speak with him about it and tried my best to approach the subject with as much gentleness as I could. I said, "Bear Heart, you seem to be having a hard time. Are you trying to decide what to do?" He gave me his little side-of-the-mouth smile that said, "that's amusing." I took a breath and said, "Do you want to stay, or do you want to go?" He looked thoughtful and replied, "I'd like to stay, but I have to go."

I was concerned that he might pass on his granddaughter Katie's birthday, August 5. She had been particularly close to him as a very young child and is named after Bear Heart's mom, her great grandmother. I also feared that he might leave on my own birthday later in the month. I was ruminating about the possibilities of meaningful dates he might choose. Some spiritual leader elders have been known to pass on a particular day they have chosen.

Bear Heart passed on the morning of August 4, 2008. I stopped thinking about the date because there was so much to do. His niece, Minisa Crumbo Halsey from Oklahoma, was there with us and had used her Eagle fan to "fan him off" the night before he left. I knew she had helped him pass peacefully. When she offered to drive me and Bear Heart's grandson, Bobby Charcoal, to Okemah, Oklahoma, for the funeral, I didn't hesitate to say, "Yes, thank you." Minisa was very close to Bear Heart, and I was very grateful that she took the reins that day.

I had already made arrangements for Bear Heart's body to be flown to Oklahoma City and transported to Okemah, where he was born. He was to be buried next to Edna, his wife of 54 years, and their son, Marc Nathan Williams, who died in a plane accident while serving in the Coast Guard on special duty. He was 17 years old.

On the drive to Oklahoma from New Mexico, my mind was occupied with thoughts of what I might have forgotten. Did I have the right shirt, the right Bolo tie? Bear Heart wanted Reverend Jimmy Anderson, the man who had been close to him in the church, to give the eulogy. I think he was in his late 80s and had recently been in an auto accident. He was recovering, but I had no assurance he could make the trip from his home in Oklahoma City. Another concern was that my Mohawk sister, Sunny Drew, was coming from Virginia to help do the cooking. Would I have enough funds to feed over 100 people?

As Bear Heart's niece Minisa was driving, she kept talking to Bobby and me about an event on the Mayan Calendar. I couldn't relate to what she was saying, so I just kept going through the list of responsibilities I had taken on. She said something about higher consciousness and those who would ascend. I always had a lot of respect for Minisa as a teacher. I didn't interrupt her but kept to my thoughts of what I needed to do so the funeral would go well. I think Bobby had fallen asleep in the back seat, and I was worried about him because his grandparents were like parents to him.

When the funeral day arrived, August 8, 2008, I realized what Minisa was speaking about. That was the Day of Ascension of Higher

Consciousness on the Mayan Indian Calendar. I knew Bear Heart never did anything haphazardly; he had a way of knowing what was needed and would comply with his Creator no matter what. My answer to what he was intending by hanging on to life was clear. By passing on August 4 and knowing his tribal ways, he would have to be buried on the fourth day, which turned out to be (08/08/08). He was buried peacefully, on the Mayan Day of Ascension of Higher Consciousness, as he had planned.

The night before Bear Heart crossed over, he went into detail about each person who had come to give him healings and blessings. He kept thanking me for all the good care he received; he would say, "You not only took care of me, but you took care of and cooked for my little family." That is how he described his daughter, Mari, six grandchildren, and one great-grandchild, Ambrose (age five at the time). His gratefulness went on and on, and I tried to stay present and let him express himself. At last, he said something that made me realize he was no longer speaking to me. He said, "I don't know what you have in store for me, but I am willing." He was still looking straight into my eyes, but those last words, I am sure, were meant for his Creator, not me. Bear Heart passed just as he had lived—grateful and willing.

A while after Bear Heart passed, the movie *Lincoln* came out. Bear Heart had always made it clear that despite some issues, President Lincoln was one of his main heroes, and he knew a lot about him. I wanted to see the movie by myself because I suspected that I was going to learn something and needed to really focus. I wanted to experience it as fully as possible.

When Lincoln was with his Cabinet buddies having a good conversation, he was being pressured to get ready to go to the theatre on that fateful evening. As he put on his overcoat, he said, "I'd like to stay, but I have to go," and smiled at the fellows. I was shocked, and a belly laugh began to bubble up in me. That Bear Heart! He was quoting Lincoln to me when I had struggled with asking him the sensitive question about his deciding when to pass on. As always, he crafted his answers to be more than frivolous.

CHAPTER 17

HIS 90-YEAR EARTH WALK

— Reginah WaterSpirit —

Bear Heart accomplished much in his 90-year Earth walk, in large part because he did not see differences among people as barriers. His training in the traditions of his Native Muscogee Creek Tribe and as a Baptist Minister, and his service as a Native American Church Road Man, enhanced the healing path of himself and those around him. He felt compassion for anyone who entered his life asking for help and "Never met a stranger." As a result, his legacy today stretches widely into the lives and cultures of many people.

I witnessed the evolution of many groups—circles of love—that he blessed with his vision of people living with unconditional trust in a loving higher power. Two, in particular, have developed their own very individualized identity, and they both continue strongly to this day.

The first is an Earth-based spiritual community, the Earthtribe, that began in the early 80s. The co-founders were Will Taegel, PhD (of Shawnee heritage), and his spouse, Dr. Judith Yost. It was born of Will's years of vision questing with Bear Heart and leading quests himself. For over 35 years, this purposeful community has grown, with members now all over the world. It is based on Bear Heart and

Will Taegel's commitment to bringing people back to nature to heal their bodies, minds, and spirits.

The Earthtribe holds an event, the Earth Dance, every October, and participants sign up a year in advance to lead eco-dramas. The qualities of the eight directions and their specific fields of energy and purpose are honored. Although these activities are specific to the Earthtribe, Bear Heart's influence is always felt and spoken about by leaders and others who knew him.

The other initiative cherished by Bear Heart is called the Gathering of Circles, established in 1995 when Cliff "Winter Fox" Buchanan and Mike "Three Bears" Andrews asked Bear Heart to be the first keynote speaker. Many Gathering of Circles events were held over the years that followed, all on top of the Sacramento Mountains near Cloudcroft, New Mexico. One of their purposes is to bring groups of people together who meet and celebrate in their respective communities.

There is always a keynote speaker selected by the elders of the gathering, and there are workshops, sweat lodge ceremonies, a dance (which is the high point for the gathering), songs, poems, and stories, all things that Bear Heart encouraged people to do. Bear Heart returned as the main speaker for the 10th anniversary, and after he passed, I recreated one of his workshops at a Gathering of Circles near Cloudcroft, New Mexico, to honor him as an ancestor of the event.

I picture the Gathering of Circles like families from Bear Heart's childhood town, coming together to pray, learn, and celebrate nature, with the difference being that here all religious beliefs were honored, and a broader love is projected for all the Earth's people.

BEAR HEART:
THE CONTINUING JOURNEY

— Doug Alderson —

Born in Okemah, Oklahoma, Grandfather Bear Heart Marcellus Williams was first trained in the medicine ways of his people, the Muscogee Creek, and later in the ways of many other traditions. Through talks, ceremonies, and healing practices, he touched thousands of people in positive ways. One example of his continuing presence among us is in his writings. First, we had *The Wind is My Mother*, widely read and translated into 14 different languages, and now we have been gifted with *The Bear Is My Father*, written in the last years of his life.

While some medicine people never leave their home region, one of Bear Heart's teachers told him that his medicine would take him around the world. This prophecy indeed proved true. Over the course of his life, Bear Heart freely shared his healing gifts and wisdom with people of all cultures and backgrounds, often traveling to different regions of the United States and to other countries. He upheld the tenet that a true medicine person is equitable in his or her practices, and his example of tolerance and acceptance is one we can all emulate.

Bear Heart was gifted in revealing the common denominator in different beliefs and in knowing what people needed to learn. In reflecting upon his passing, I recalled that after one profound experience with Bear Heart, one in which I had an out-of-body type of experience, I began to understand why spiritual people begin to lose their fear of death. There is freedom in being unencumbered by the body. One could even look forward to the transition of death if the time has come when the body is weighed down with suffering and one's purpose on Earth is fulfilled. "Before you can have the Great

Power," Bear Heart told me soon afterward, "you must have that dependency on God—that surrendering. Then you can get into the realm of no limitations."

Most who knew Bear Heart will remember him as a human being with a big heart, a hearty laugh, an overflowing sense of compassion, and someone who could cut through anything with truth. He used his powerful gifts and knowledge to guide and help heal many people, including myself. He taught me humility and the power of prayer, and I always sensed that he foresaw my potential before I realized it. Most importantly, he inspired me to travel to the Source for truth and guidance.

Reginah WaterSpirit-Williams, Bear Heart's medicine helper and late-life companion remarked that people who read Bear Heart's writing just start feeling better and become more optimistic. I think when reading Bear Heart's words, you will agree. And the writings of his close associates and family members included in this book have revealed more insights about this gifted teacher, father, and grandfather.

I was pleased that when my book *The Vision Keepers* was nearing publication, Reginah read excerpts to him, and he gave it his full blessing. He was never far from my heart, and he will be deeply missed. Grandfather Bear Heart Marcellus Williams made his transition into Spirit on Monday, August 4, 2008, at the age of 90.

But will Bear Heart be completely gone? Does the wind ever stop and not return?

❧ ❧ ❧

Perhaps Bear Heart's greatest legacy exists in the minds and hearts he touched all over the world: Native American Church Roadmen to whom he "gave his fireplace" (taught his ceremonial ways); people he guided as they went on spirit quests; members of the two groups described above; folks who heard him talk, read his book, or saw him in a video; and those who received his counsel and attended his ceremonies. There are many who still call him "grandfather," people he considered to be family. He saw the whole world as family.

Bear Heart brought together Western medicine and Native American spiritual ways. He led people into cultures that were historically kept secret, which was a controversial thing among some Native people. He was one of a very few traditionally trained Native American medicine people who created those bridges into the larger world—who chose not to guard and hoard Indigenous wisdom but to share it with an open heart.

Bear Heart did not focus on his personal legacy but on the needs of others and the calls of the times. Particularly now, the stakes have become too great to ignore, and the world's need for Indigenous wisdom is great. As he would admonish us, "We don't just need to find a way to make a living; we need to learn how to live!"

He taught by the way he lived. People were influenced by his responses to his own personal challenges and tragedies. We all benefited from Bear Heart's extraordinary commitment of faith and trust in the goodness of all people and our need to live in harmony with nature, which we are a part of.

CHAPTER 18
VISION CIRCLE

— Will Taegel —

For over a decade, Bear Heart journeyed to Houston to spend extended time with me. At the time, Judith and I lived with our two daughters in a big white house in a vibrant neighborhood in the heart of Houston called Montrose. Bear Heart loved sprawling out on the couch in our living room. One late spring night, after we had been together as guides in an early Earthtribe vision quest, he spoke to me in Creek/Muscogee in a booming voice, saying, "Foswa Enhalsewah!" Then when his laughter filled the large room, I jumped in surprise.

From our many conversations, I knew this laughter was a harbinger of a deeper message and that he was calling me by a name he said came from the Sacred Mystery as part of my vision quest early in our relationship. He used the name to disturb my status quo and as a point of emphasis. It is loosely translated as "Bird Medicine." At other times, he seemed to translate the name as "Winged Medicine," a description that resonated with me. When he spoke in his tribal language, I tuned in and paid close attention. He continued:

"Everybody belongs to a clan, sometimes several clans. The purpose of the clan is to let you know that you belong. You are never alone, and the clan is there to assist you with who you are—your true identity. Your first clan is Foswalki, the bird clan.

The winged ones can take you up in the sky, past the arms of our Grandmother toward Grandfather Sun, Hasi. Pretty soon, you will find Hasi Innini, the Path of the Sun. You live in a culture where loneliness and a sense of being estranged is everywhere present. Your patients are depressed and anxious because they don't know that their clan brothers and sisters follow them around just over their left shoulder. It's funny; the mainstream drowns in a sea of loneliness, what you called alienation the other day. All the while, their clan is there to help them see just how connected we all are, at the deepest level. We feel lonely, but we are never alone. Let's go outside under the stars. I am going to teach you a song that can lead you to Hasi Innini. It is a Comanche song to the eagle:

> *Quena, yo wa kno,*
> *Yanna hey,*
> *Quena, yo wa kno*
> *Yanna hey,*
> *Quena, yo wa know*
> *Yanna hey,*
> *Hey ya wanna*
> *Hey ya wanna,*
> *Hey hey yo wey."*

Bear Heart looked up to the stars, and I sensed he wanted to tell me something more as if he was receiving a hidden variable from the splash of stars, visible even in the night sky of an urban setting. "The flap of wings lead you higher to Sun's Path."

His words deeply resonated with me, yet I could not translate them into my life at that time. Time cycled through a couple of decades. Two years after he stepped through the big door to travel beyond the stars, I lay beside a lake in a vision circle. The stars reflected off the waters and reached into my heart, and I knew that was what he was telling me that night he taught me to fly with the eagles. He saw something in my heart, stars perhaps, that I didn't yet grasp myself. He saw a link to the stars, the gateway to the larger perspective so needed in a world divided.

Let me reflect for a moment. Bear Heart was a layered human, complex in many ways. Perhaps, finding simplicity and clarity to balance his complexity enabled him to envision the possibility of a larger identity as he guided vision quests. I don't know if he spoke in Creek/Muscogee regularly with others, but he often did with me. He sometimes wrote me notes in his mother tongue. In the early days of the Earthtribe, he gave me translations of the vision names seekers were receiving in both English and Creek/Muscogee.

I didn't become facile in that language, but I learned enough to know that, in many ways, it was congruent with what I was learning and teaching. It was the auspicious 20th-century physicist David Bohm who said, "The verb-oriented language of the Indigenous people is the closest I have found to quantum physics." I found that to be true of Bear Heart's native tongue.

Later, I would write a book called *The Mother Tongue* that linked ancient wisdom and eco-field physics. Until this very moment, I didn't realize its roots went back to the night Bear Heart looked at the stars and sang of wings in the sky and the path of the Sun. In many ways, it was the lilt of his Native tongue that, even today, inspires and gently guides me.

CHAPTER 19

STAR GAZING

— Reginah WaterSpirit —

One day in 2012, I received an email from a fellow I did not know, Herb MacDonald, a man who had read a book by Bear Heart and had an important message for him. I had to tell Herb that Bear Heart had passed on in 2008, but I thanked him for his story which is particularly touching for me because Bear Heart believed with all his heart in a Star Nation. The Star Nation is referred to by many cultures of Native Americans in their creation stories. Here it is:

BEAR HEART'S SON

— Herb MacDonald —

There was a horrific crash only one month before I was scheduled to return stateside for my last assignment in the US Air Force. It was Monday evening, May 11, 1964. At around 7:30 pm, it was announced that a plane had crashed short of the runway, and any emergency personnel should return to their assigned area. Before getting a cab back to the hospital, I was able to observe the fire and smoke through the mist, as a thunderstorm had just passed through the area.

Upon returning to the hospital, I was assigned to an ambulance that transported several of us to the disaster site. It was at least 45 minutes after the crash that we arrived at the site. The fire was out, there was no smoke, and searchlights had been set up. Search and rescue had already been there, and it turned out that we had become part of the recovery operation. My first task was to assist in recovering the several charred bodies, which were burned beyond recognition. We placed each body on a litter and lifted them onto the bed of a box truck. There was enough room for only eight or ten casualties due to their rigid outstretched limbs.

When that task was completed, we focused on the remaining individuals. One by one, we performed our grim assignment. However, one body, in particular, lingers in my mind. No matter how severe and gruesome those first burned bodies might have assaulted my young psyche, this young airman in his dress blues (at that time, I thought he was an airman) was still fastened to his seat. He and his whole seat assembly had been wrenched from the fuselage of the jet, which was strewn about in three sections far from the end of the runway. This young man and his seat came to rest among the remains scattered about in the field. There he was, lying in his seat facing upward as if gazing at the stars. What particularly lingers in my mind when I think back on this scene is his total absence of apparent injury. He was a young dark-skinned serviceman in uniform with one stripe on his left sleeve, about my own age (he was only 17 years old), bearing the name tag of "Williams" upon his chest.

When I unfastened his seatbelt, I recall a distinct pop, as if he had been distended. I will always reflect on the fact that I undid his last effort to keep himself safe as we lifted him out of his seat and eased him into the body bag. Among all the desolation of that crash site, this isolated seat containing a spotless, seemingly unharmed airman has had the greatest impact on me over all these years.

I first read *The Wind Is My Mother* in 1997, written by Bear Heart. It was the dedication page that captivated my attention:

"This book is lovingly dedicated to my personal hero, who died in the Philippines on May 11th, 1964, while in the service of our country—my son, Marc Nathan Williams. B.H."

It was at that moment when I made the link between this dedication and my participation in the recovery operation on that day while I served in the Philippines.

When I began reading Bear Heart's book, I was unaware of the coincidence that I had been present at the crash site where Bear Heart's son had died. I did not make the connection until later when I learned that Bear Heart's legal name was Marcellus Williams. At that point, I remembered the name tag on the young man I released from the seat that was thrown free of the wrecked plane. I realized that he may well have been Bear Heart's son.

For some reason I cannot explain why I had a burning desire to contact Bear Heart to see if there was a way to find out if I did, indeed, play a part in caring for his son after his tragic death. It's like I had a need for Bear Heart to know that his son was respectfully treated. I wanted him to know the life-long effect on another young man, me, which has not been and never will be forgotten. I felt like I had a cosmic connection of some sort with Bear Heart, along with a feeling that I needed to share this intense experience.

When I entertained the thought of contacting Bear Heart, there was great apprehension as to how I would introduce myself—what purpose would it serve, and how would I go about it? These thoughts just lingered on the back burner.

Finally, after reading about Bear Heart on the internet, I was able to make contact with Reginah WaterSpirit on July 4, 2012. We had a conversation that spanned more than an hour and forty minutes. This turned out to be one of the most satisfying and enlightening discussions I ever had.

Since my first conversation with Reginah, I have learned that Marc Nathan Williams was not in the Air Force as I had presumed in 1964 but was a Seaman Apprentice in the US Coast Guard. With the ability to search Coast Guard insignia on the internet, I was able to see how easy it was for me to confuse the two uniforms fifty years ago. I recall an odd sensation so long ago when I helped remove Marc from his seat that his single slanted stripe was unlike the airman's single chevron. I was unfamiliar with Coast Guard uniforms at that early time in my life. After all, I was in the Air Force; this was an Air Force base and an Air force jet that had crashed. It seemed logical to me at that time that Marc was a young airman like myself.

Bear Heart, who touched the lives of many people with his insights and mutual respect, imbued his listeners with their responsibility to care for one another. He made it his mission to impart to all of us that we have the distinct accountability to care for Mother Earth. I feel honored that I had an opportunity, however limited, to care for his personal hero, his son Marc Nathan.

❦ ❦ ❦

Whenever I think about this story, it reminds me of the circles of love that surrounded Bear Heart. I like to imagine Bear Heart's son when Herb found him, open eyes pointed toward Ursa Major, the great bear constellation, his spirit having said to his beloved father, "I will wait for you there."

Tim Amsden: I grew up in Wichita, Kansas, obtained a law degree, and worked 25 years for the US Environmental Protection Agency in Kansas City. As a writer, I am mostly a poet, with work published in the US and elsewhere. A volume of my poetry was published in 2015, and I have recently completed a book about living in the wilds of Ramah, New Mexico, with my wife, Lucia. The book, *Love Letter to Ghost Land,* focuses on New Mexico's deep and exotic sense of place and the necessity of embracing our existence as part of nature that is inherent in the spiritual beliefs of Native people. Lucia and I had been friends with Bear Heart and Reginah for many years, and when they offered me the honor of editing this book, I eagerly accepted. That process has led us into many experiences and times with them and immeasurably enriched our lives.

Mike Three Bears Andrews: My name is Mike Andrews, but I go by Mike Three Bears, one of several names Bear Heart gave over the 19 years I knew and worked with him. I met him in 1997 and attended many purification (sweat) lodges, vision quests, Native American Church prayer services, and other ceremonies until his passing in the summer of 2008. In 2004, he authorized me to sponsor and lead vision quests in his tradition, which I continue to do today. I have a Bachelor of Science and a Master of Science degree in chemical engineering from New Mexico State University in Las Cruces, New Mexico. After a career in the corporate world, I got a certificate to teach high school science, which I did on a reservation west of Albuquerque, New Mexico. I have lived in Taos, New Mexico, for 23 years.

Bob Bergman, MD: I grew up and was educated in Chicago and knew little or nothing about Native Americans; I thought the Navajos lived in the Dakotas.

I would have stayed all my life in Chicago except for the Vietnam War when instead of being drafted, I signed up for two years in the US Public Health Service. I was given a brochure that listed the various divisions of the service, and the Division of Indian Health looked the most interesting, so I asked to be assigned there. I was sent to the Navajo Nation and two years turned into ten because I loved being there, immersed in the culture, especially in traditional Navajo medicine, religion, and the Native American Church. I was profoundly changed as a person and a doctor, and I am thankful for that opportunity.

Nina Brown: After moving from Philadelphia, Pennsylvania, to Santa Fe, New Mexico, I found a job at the Los Alamos Medical Center. As the story I wrote for this book tells the reader, that is where I magically met Bear Heart. I would say "The Dance of the Universe" brought us together. We became friends, as I did with his wife, Reginah, sharing meals, conversations, laughter, and sweat lodges. My life is richer because of our experiences together, as are my memories.

Lisa Costlow: Lisa was born in Wichita, Kansas, to a family with Citizen Band Potawatomi, Welsh, and Irish heritage, and was the owner of a successful Aveda concept salon and spa for 11 years. A deep desire to help others drew her to the study of Ayurveda and a number of other healing modalities, including Reiki, homeopathy, and traditional Indigenous practices. Her integrative approach has given her a unique appreciation for the role of culture in the healing process and enhanced her work with people from many cultural backgrounds in a respectful and compassionate way.

Walter Dominguez: Walter Dominguez is a southern California-born and raised filmmaker. He is a second-generation Latino/Hispanic of Mexican and Spanish heritage. In 1973, Walter met noted stage, television, and film actress, Shelley Morrison, and they wed that same year. In the early 1980s, Walter took a long break from television and film to learn about Native American spirituality and ritual after meeting and being mentored by Muscogee Creek spiritual elder Bear Heart Williams. Along with his wife Shelley, they traveled around the country, assisting Bear Heart and participating in numerous ceremonies. In 2002, Walter and Shelley formed a production company, Chasing Light Pictures LLC, in order to make cross-border and multicultural documentaries. Shelley executive produced, and Walter wrote, directed, and produced their acclaimed documentary feature film, *Weaving the Past: Journey of Discovery*, released in 2014. Walter is currently in production on a public television history series, *Whitewashed Adobe: The Rise of Los Angeles*. Walter and Shelley were married until her passing in December 2019.

Bev Doolittle: Bev Doolittle is celebrated for her paintings that reflect her passion for horses, the natural world, and Native American spiritual reverence for the living earth. She is particularly noted for the aspect in her work that she describes as "camouflage technique," whereby some details appear to be one thing but, when examined more closely, are seen to be something else as well. Thus, for instance, a cluster of stones may also be a bear or bison, or close examination of a snow-dappled hillside may reveal the image of an Indian mounted on a pinto pony. In addition to prints of her paintings, five books of her art have been published. She has also released three children's books, one book for young readers, and created five limited edition porcelain boxes—each featuring one of her most popular paintings. Bev and her husband, Jay, began married life as art directors for a Los Angeles advertising agency but eventually struck out on their own, traveling and painting through the Western United States and Canada. Today, her paintings are beloved around the world, not only for their artistic quality but for their expression of the unity of humans with the earth and its other life forms. In her words, "My love for nature, as well as man's relationship with it, is the driving force behind all my artwork."

Pat Embers: Northern Ohio near Lake Erie was where I grew up in a small town, and my interest in healing led me to become an occupational therapist. Cultural interests took me to Lyon, France, where Ken, a linguist, and English as a second language teacher from Kansas, came into my life. We came back to Manhattan, Kansas, married, and have a daughter, Sheila, who is now an apparel designer. My cultural and Earth-loving ways kept growing, and in 1998, I found Bear Heart at a Medicine Wheel Gathering. I invited both him and Reginah WaterSpirit to our Flint Hills prairie land. Bear Heart's workshops on Native Earth spirituality, sweat lodge ceremonies, and vision quests brought Spirit into rural Kansas communities. His inspiration of Native ways led me in 2001 to join the Wisdom Keepers Conference staff in Council Grove, Kansas, and eventually, I became a Sun Dancer. Our 2020 Flint Hills Wisdom Keepers Foundation Board (fhwisdomkeepers.org) continues sponsoring annual gatherings led by Native American elders that have included knowledge shared by both Bear Heart and Reginah WaterSpirit. To this day, I honor Bear Heart in my home sweat lodge, grateful for his loving and shared gifts of harmony with Great Spirit, Mother Earth, and All Our Relations.

Herb MacDonald: I was born and raised in Worcester, Massachusetts. Eventually, I enlisted in the US Air Force with my best high school buddy, T.L., and trained as a medic. I served two years in the Philippines, and my last tour of duty was at Maxwell Air Force Base in Montgomery, Alabama, where I met Mary Kilgannon, nurse and my future wife. We had in common personal experiences regarding Martin Luther King Jr. and the Civil Rights March from Selma to Montgomery in 1965. We married in Carbondale, PA., and raised two fine young men in Coatesville, PA: Martin, a software project manager, and Joseph, a physician. We were blessed with six grandchildren: Shea, Ian, Riley, Caitlin, Sydney, and Brody. I taught school for 14 years, six of which were an environmental education program for sophomores and seniors. Both Mary and I worked at the Devereaux Foundation for about 20 years, caring for individuals with behavioral, developmental, and mental challenges. I enjoy reading and photography. I most enjoyed my last six years of employment with Men's Warehouse, driving a truck delivering tuxedoes and suits to stores in a 200-mile radius of Westchester, PA. I lost Mary after 53 years of marriage in December 2019.

Rev. Neal Rzepkowski, MD: I grew up near Lily Dale, NY, a spiritualist community with over 40 mediums. When I was a teen, my first reading with a medium predicted that I would end up as a doctor, which was far from my mind. But it happened! On my journey of studying mediumship and spirituality, including through medical school, I met Reginah and Bear Heart at Bear Tribe Medicine Wheel gatherings. I invited Bear Heart to Lily Dale, where he did workshops and sweat lodges for several summers.

Robert Seidenspinner: I am a relationship/systems coach, teacher, father, and grandfather. I live in Northern California with my wife, Beth Ann. I am also a singer of Native American Church songs and a long-time adopted nephew of Bear Heart.

Will Taegel, PhD: Bear Heart and I met at a conference of The American Academy of Psychotherapists, where he enlisted me to assist with an informal healing ceremony for psychologists and psychiatrists. As a mixed-blood with a Shawnee grandparent and a child of the Llano Estacado of Northwest Texas who cut his teeth on Quanah Parker, I had a natural inclination to Indigenous wisdom. On the other hand, a PhD in eco-psychology filled me with questions. What followed was a 28 year friendship and collaboration. Like elder and younger brothers, we loved and also frustrated each other. Beyond the ups and downs, we joined hands in the birthing of an important Earth-based community—the Earthtribe—which is vibrant to this day. Our relationship yielded an integration of ancient wisdom and the newer sciences, including what came to be known as eco-therapy. We had not spoken in a while when Bear Heart asked Reginah WaterSpirit to summon me to New Mexico. In what was a soul-stirring reunion for both of us, we achieved an intimacy that I will carry with me always. A few weeks later, Bear Heart stepped through the great door to the stars and beyond. In a miracle of consciousness, he still visits in many of our dreams and continues a generosity of heart.

Doug Alderson: My vision quest was a 2,000-mile hike on the Appalachian Trail at age 18, whereupon I understood my life would be about working towards environmental protection and appreciation and embracing a Native American path. This led to my involvement with Bear Heart four years later, where he adopted me as his nephew, a traditional teaching relationship. Bear Heart taught me many things about the earth and native ways and how to help others. Subsequently, I worked as a naturalist, environmental advocate, outdoor guide, wildlife magazine editor, and trail planner. I am now in my mid-60s and still draw upon those early lessons with Bear Heart as I follow a path as a writer and leader at a Muscogee Creek ceremonial grounds in North Florida.

ACKNOWLEDGMENTS

Support to create and complete *The Bear Is My Father,* a book that Bear Heart and I began over 20 years ago, came from all the sacred directions. Nature herself gave me clues for the proper timing to pursue this labor of love, testing my patience. Creative editors with heart and spirit, open-hearted community members, and our publisher's skillful team member's guidance are all essential elements that came together to complete this book. M'do, thank you to the following people who made this journey meaningful and joy-filled for me.

Thank you, Tim and Lucia Amsden. When Bear Heart and I first visited your home in Ramah, New Mexico, in 2005, your open hearts created an atmosphere for wondrous travels in creativity. You, Tim, became our chief editor. Lucia, a wise and connected woman, became my confidant and spiritual rock, the keeper of soulfulness for the many aspects of this project. Your sisterly support made it possible for my true voice to be heard. The talents of you both in the field of writing and publishing have honored Bear Heart's story with integrity that touches my heart. I am grateful for your gifts of tenacious attention to detail, especially honoring Bear Heart's way of speaking, as his first language was that of his Creek tribe. You helped me expand the project after Bear Heart passed, providing a unique approach for this work. I am so grateful that you both never fail to bring joyful laughter into any session of work. M'do, Thank you.

Thank you, Sidra Stone, and our ancestral relative, Hal Stone. Your unconditional kindness and introduction to fluid paradigms made way for me to birth this book with Bear Heart. Truth be told, you made way for my entire journey into Bear Heart's world and ownership of my own.

Thank you, Steven Sachs, *Muqit*, our ceremonial chief in New Mexico. Your insight into realms of love gave me the energy to keep moving in a hopeful way. Your blessings, backed by "frogskins" when needed, gave me the space to witness a new landscape in which to be grateful. I am in awe of the scope of your generosity.

Thank you, Will *Star Heart* Taegel, Mekko, chief of our Earthtribe and friend to Bear Heart, for calling this book a "sister" to your thought-provoking book, *Walking with Bears, On Bridges to Earth's New Era*. Your council on this project, as we took it from notes to a meaningful collaboration, has brought me joyful intimacy with our community. Your knowledgeable spirited contributions have been beyond generous.

Thank you, 2nd Tier Publishing, Dan Gauthier, *Rock Brother*, and Shiila Safer, *Winged Birthing*, for your unselfish support to secure the greatest potential for this book's success. Your ability to hold visions for other members of our species has no boundaries, only love.

Thank you, Madoh, Lille Rowden, Wise Wind, for always being there to raise the vibration to smiles and laughter or deeper thought. As a wise elder of our Earthtribe, your friendship and guidance for me and my projects are treasured. Your long "her-story" with our beloved Bear Heart ties us together in spirit and life.

Thank you, my Brothers and Sisters of our Earthtribe, *Ennake*, cherished relatives. These last 13 years with all of you have given nourishment for my soul and made a path for a deeper appreciation of our Earth Mother, our home.

Thank you, Todah Rabah, Jonathan Feinn, my thoughtful and heartwarming friend. When I found you a few years after Bear Heart passed, you encouraged my journey toward clarity in my writing. Your gifts of perception helped me say what I mean. You are a true friend. I treasure you.

Thank you, Jerry Patchen, Esq., *Red Hawk*, for connecting me with Synergetic Press. Thank you, M'do, for your gracious manner as you make far-reaching contributions to all whose paths you come across. When I think of you, I see you sitting in the tipi with Bear Heart, in prayer for all of us and our precious home place, Earth.

Thank you, Doug Reil, of Synergetic Press. From the very beginning, you brought to my attention the specialness of this book. Your skillful communications with me and especially with our editor-in-chief, Tim Amsden, brought our book to new levels of professional excellence. I am in awe of your support and appreciation of sacredness as we worked to maintain Bear Heart's legacy. I feel blessed by the grace of your guidance to help this book's message reach the hearts of many. Todah Rabah.

Thank you, Rabbi Aryel Nachman ben Chaim, brother, and friend of Bear Heart and mentor, guide, and fellow puppeteer of mine. Your deep appreciation of Bear Heart's own connection to the 12 tribes bound our hearts to yours and your family forever. Your skill in translating Creek and other American Indian words and expressions into Hebrew for us in Bear Heart's first book, *The Wind Is My Mother*, was so special and will hopefully be needed again when this volume is published in Hebrew.

Thank you, Bev Doolittle. Over the many years, your and Jay's experience as writers and editors has inspired me to continue my efforts to share Bear Heart's and my stories. Bev, your paintings, inspired by Nature, gave Bear Heart and me much joy. As I wrote my part in this book, I often thought of how you helped me to have a keener eye for detail. Your presence in my life has blessed all that I endeavor to create.

Thank you, Lawry Swidler and Ulla Darni of upstate New York. Your devotion to your connection with ancestral Bear Heart is so inspiring for me and a force in the creation of this book. Your dedication to his and my well-being on many levels for over two decades continues to teach me how genuine humility can heal what ails. A very heartfelt, Madoh, thank you both.

My mother, Ruth Boettcher, would tell people that her middle child, Reginah, was born with a crayon in her mouth. Because of her confidence in my artistic abilities, I have never veered far from a creative life. All the accomplishments in my life have her blessing on them, and I am beyond grateful. Todah Rabah, mom.

I also give thanks to my dad, Jasper Yurman, who would not have been deterred by the need to take 20 years to finish a project. I inherited my "perseverance gene" from him. Todah Rabah, dad.

Thank you, Bear Heart's and my late doggies, Misha, Blankah Krypto and Tahlequah, and Rocky Mountain, who is still with me, for tolerating delayed walks and giving all your love to both of us during challenging times and good. Without your presence and devoted trust in me, the project spoken of here might have fallen by the wayside. The four of you have been and are my special treats.

❧ ❧ ❧

The whole is greater than the sum of the parts, some say. Without the contributions from these good people and our furry family, this book would not be here.

— **Reginah WaterSpirit**